Walter E. Crum

The Amherst Papyri

Being an account of the Egyptian papyri in the collection of the Right Hon.

Lord Amherst of Hackney, F.S.A. at Didlington Hall, Norfolk

Walter E. Crum

The Amherst Papyri
Being an account of the Egyptian papyri in the collection of the Right Hon. Lord Amherst of Hackney, F.S.A. at Didlington Hall, Norfolk

ISBN/EAN: 9783337243302

Printed in Europe, USA, Canada, Australia, Japan

Cover: Foto ©ninafisch / pixelio.de

THE AMHERST PAPYRI,

BEING AN ACCOUNT OF

THE EGYPTIAN PAPYRI IN THE COLLECTION OF
THE RIGHT HON. LORD AMHERST OF HACKNEY, F.S.A.,

AT

DIDLINGTON HALL, NORFOLK,

BY

PERCY E. NEWBERRY.

WITH

AN APPENDIX ON A COPTIC PAPYRUS,

BY

W. E. CRUM, M.A.

WITH TWENTY-FOUR AUTOTYPE PLATES.

LONDON
BERNARD QUARITCH, 15, PICCADILLY, W.
1899.

HARRISON AND SONS,
PRINTERS IN ORDINARY TO HER MAJESTY,
ST. MARTIN'S LANE, LONDON.

TO

THE RIGHT HONOURABLE

VISCOUNT CROMER,

G.C.B., G.C.M.G., K.C.S.I., C.I.E.,

HER BRITANNIC MAJESTY'S AGENT AND CONSUL-GENERAL

IN

EGYPT,

AND A MINISTER PLENIPOTENTIARY IN HER MAJESTY'S DIPLOMATIC SERVICE,

THIS VOLUME,

WHICH HAS BEEN COMPILED IN ACCORDANCE WITH THE DESIRE EXPRESSED BY HIS LORDSHIP,
THAT THE CONTENTS OF THE PAPYRI EXISTING IN PRIVATE COLLECTIONS IN
THIS COUNTRY, AS WELL AS OF THOSE IN PUBLIC MUSEUMS,
SHOULD BE MADE KNOWN FOR THE BENEFIT
OF STUDENTS OF EGYPTIAN
ANTIQUITIES,

IS MOST RESPECTFULLY

DEDICATED.

PREFACE.

The title of this volume, "*An Account of the Egyptian Papyri in the Collection of Lord Amherst of Hackney*," sufficiently explains its purport.

I wish here to acknowledge my sincerest thanks to Lord and Lady Amherst, for having allowed me to delay the publication of this book for many months. Its preparation has required much preliminary study, and has necessitated my reading through most of the ancient documents already published, as well as many of those preserved in the Museums of Europe and Egypt, which are, as yet, unpublished.

The proofs have been read through by my friend Wilhelm Spiegelberg, Professor of Egyptology in the University of Strassburg, but, of course, he is in no way responsible for any errors that may be found in the work; to him I wish to express my gratitude for much help and many valuable suggestions.

PERCY E. NEWBERRY.

October 1st, 1899.

CONTENTS.

INTRODUCTION.

The treasures of Egyptian Art and Literature gathered together by Lord and Lady Amherst of Hackney, and preserved at Didlington Hall, Norfolk, form, if not the most extensive, one of the most important, private collections of the kind in this country. Many of the objects are of unique interest. The series of mummy cases, the bronzes, the amulets and ushabti figures are particularly noteworthy, and the collection of monuments from the historic site of Tell el Amarna is of unsurpassed interest. But there is another class of antiquities at Didlington Hall which is perhaps the most important of the whole collection: it is the series of Egyptian papyri dating from the Middle Kingdom period of Egyptian history (*circa* 2500 B.C.) and extending down to Arab times.

The nucleus of this valuable collection of papyri was the small series, numbering some five documents, formed by the late Dr. Lee and purchased by Lord Amherst of Hackney, with the entire collection of that learned Doctor, about the year 1868. From that date till the present time it has been gradually added to, and now there are some two hundred different papyri in the Didlington Hall museum. The collection includes not merely the religious documents which are so common in museums, but literary, legal and other papyri. It comprises specimens of Hieroglyphic, Hieratic and Demotic writing, as well as of Greek, Coptic and Arabic. Of these, twenty Demotic and Greek papyri of the second century B.C. were found together in an earthenware jar near Thebes; three of the Demotic documents contain dockets written in Greek, and these may be expected to be of considerable help in the decipherment of the Demotic character.

The Amherst papyri are of very great importance for several reasons; among them are certain fragments which enable us to complete, or partially complete, documents in other collections. Others there are which, complete or almost so in themselves, contain references to persons and events recorded in papyri and monuments in other collections. The series of chapters from the Book of the Dead, of which there are parts of copies made for no less than twenty-four individuals, is also of considerable interest, containing as it does some eighty-four chapters.

THE AMHERST PAPYRI.

I.

Papyri Nos. I, II and IV are fragments of a series of early literary documents discovered many years ago in some locality, perhaps Thebes, in Upper Egypt. The main part of the "find" was brought to England in 1840, where it was purchased by Prof. Lepsius for the Berlin Museum, and the papyri of which it was composed (four in number) were soon after (in 1842) published by him in fac-simile. The first of these, known as the Berlin Papyrus No. I, contains the celebrated story of Sanehat, and describes the fate of an exile among the Syrian bedawin. The tale is simple and homely, and written in a semi-poetic style. It was one of the most popular of ancient Egyptian stories, and was widely read for centuries, a copy of part of it having been written as late as the XXth dynasty (*circa* 1000 B.C.).

The second and fourth papyri of the Berlin series contain copies of one and the same tale, which is also very simple in character. It tells of a quarrel between a peasant and a townsman, which purports to have happened at Henenseten or Herakleopolis, now Ahnas, a little south of the Fayum. The third papyrus of the series (Berlin Papyrus No. III) contains a remarkable dialogue between a man and his ghost. Curiously enough, although the papyri are of great length, not one of these four documents is complete; they all want the outer coils or more of the rolls. There are fragments of three of these papyri (Berlin Nos. I, II and IV) in the Amherst Collection. When and where Lord Amherst procured them is unfortunately not certain, but it seems probable that they were obtained with the collections of Mr. Lieder of Cairo in the year 1861. An account of the fragments was published by Mr. Griffith in the *Proceedings of the Society of Biblical Archæology* for 1892, but they are published in fac-simile for the first time on Plate I of this Catalogue. They number in all sixteen pieces, of which five belong to the Berlin Papyrus No. I, five to the Berlin Papyrus No. II, and two to the Berlin Papyrus No. VI. The remaining four fragments perhaps formed part of the outer coil of No. III.

The text of the two stories contained in the Berlin Papyri Nos. I, II and IV, has been transcribed from the original documents in the Berlin Museum, and translations of them have been made by several Egyptologists. For the beginning of the tale of Sanehat the reader is referred to Prof. Maspero's publication of the XXth dynasty ostraca in the 1st *Memoir of the Institut Égyptien of Cairo*, and to Mr. Griffith's reconstruction of the text in the style of the original from the Amherst fragments, in the *Proceedings of the Society of Biblical Archæology*, Vol. XIV. The text of the Berlin Papyrus No. I is best transcribed in Prof. Maspero's edition, printed in the *Mélanges d'Archéologie Égyptienne*, III, 68, 140, but it requires considerable revision. The most trustworthy English translation of the whole story is that given in Prof. Petrie's *Egyptian Tales* (1st Series), p. 97. The Story of the Peasant has only been partially translated, and some account of it may be found in the same volume of *Egyptian Tales*, p. 61. It may be of interest to give here an outline of the two stories, the beginnings of which are preserved in the Amherst fragments.

The Tale of Sanehat tells of an Egyptian's wanderings in neighbouring lands about 2500 years before the Christian era. The Prince Usertsen, returning to Egypt from an expedition against the Libyans, is met on the road by a messenger with the news of the death of his father, the king Amenemhat I. The message is overheard by Sanehat, an officer of high position at the Egyptian court, and he is straightway driven involuntarily to take to flight. He deserts the army and travelling southwards arrives at a town called *Negau:* then, journeying in a north-easterly direction, he arrives at the frontier, which he crosses at nightfall. Overcome by hunger, thirst and fatigue, he is given food by a friendly Bedawi, who introduces him to his camp. He wanders on till he reaches *Kedem*, where he spends "half a year;" but the prince of a neighbouring land invites Sanehat to settle in his dominions. He accepts; soon gains honours and fortune and marries the prince's daughter. Sanehat, however, still retains the Egyptian's love of the land of his birth, and when advanced in years obtains permission from Usertsen, the king then reigning, to return to Egypt. He returns and is received at the Pharaoh's court with honour and presented to the queen. Sanehat concludes his life in great prosperity and is, moreover, granted the supreme blessing of a splendid sepulchre.

The Story of the Peasant, recounting a quarrel between a countryman and a townsman, is said to have been enacted at or near Henenseten or Herakleopolis, the modern Ahnas. The period must have been the IXth or Xth dynasty, when Henenseten was the seat of government. A peasant coming to market from a remote part of the country is robbed of his asses and goods by an artisan or townsman. He complains of the injustice done him before the Chief Steward Merui-tensa, and shows such courage and perseverance in his complaints that he charms the latter. The Chief Steward, indeed, is so delighted with the originality of his pleading, that, with the assent of the monarch under whom he serves, he prolongs the peasant's affair in order thus to prompt him to further discourse. In the end the peasant wins his case, his goods are given back to him together with those of the townsman, which the king has confiscated. The tale is very Egyptian in character and is most realistically and simply told.

II.

The Vth papyrus of the Collection refers to a great harem conspiracy against the life of Ramses III, of which two other documents, one in Turin and one in Paris, give us information. It appears that certain persons belonging to the royal household had conspired against the king and planned an open rebellion. As in similar cases at the present day, the harem formed the centre of the conspiracy. One of the oldest inmates Ti, had a son named Pentaur, and she with another lady of the harem conspired together with the object of placing him upon the throne. Many of the officials of the women's apartments appear also to have been inculpated in the conspiracy. Among them was the Chief Steward Pai-bak-kamen, a man of great importance to the conspirators in the harem, for through him they were enabled to correspond with the outside world. "He carried their words," runs the account, "to their mothers and brothers outside the harem." These relatives of the harem inmates were ordered to excite the people and goad on their friends to begin hostilities against the king. That they had much sympathy from the outside seems certain, as the captain of the Ethiopian troops and several other high officials are mentioned as having been won over to the conspiracy. They thought it right to use every means to do harm to the sovereign and even magic arts were invoked. It is to the trial of one of these magicians that the Amherst Papyrus No. V refers. A certain "overseer of the cattle," named Penhuiban, procured a magical roll from the king's own library, and according to directions in it he made certain wax figures and love charms which were smuggled into the palace in order to cause blindness and paralyze certain of its unfriendly inmates. Fortunately another page of this interesting document is preserved in Paris. It states that the individual who received the wax figures and charms was the Chief Steward Pai-bak-kamen. His examination before the police court is given, and it is further stated that sentence of death was passed upon him—death by his own hand. It is very interesting to note the impartiality of Pharaoh, in this case against his own person. He held altogether aloof from the trial, and as he says in the opening of the case, "as to the talk which men hold I know it not." He ordered the judges however to find out the truth, and to punish the guilty, but to beware of inflicting chastisement upon those who did not deserve it.

A study of all documents relating to the trial was published by M. Deveria in the *Journal Asiatique* for 1865,* but this translation of the Turin papyrus referring to the case has been considerably improved by Prof. Renouf in the eighth volume of the *Records of the Past* (1st Series). An account of the conspiracy has also appeared from the pen of Dr. Adolf Erman in the *Ægyptische Zeitschrift*, 1879, 76 ff. (*cf.* his *Ægypten*, p. 142).

* Reprinted in Maspero's *Bibliothèque Égyptologique*, Tome 5, pp. 97-251.

III.

Another great trial of a somewhat later period is referred to in the Amherst Papyrus No. VI. Towards the end of the XXth dynasty (about 1100 B.C.), it appears that the police authorities of Thebes had great difficulty in preventing the tombs of the western necropolis from being entered by bands of robbers, and their contents from being stolen. Several documents relating to the work of the police at the time are preserved, which throw considerable light upon the way crime was tracked, and how the trials of suspected persons were conducted. Among them the most interesting is that known as the Abbott Papyrus, in the British Museum, which was purchased in 1856 by the Trustees of that institution from Dr. Abbott of Cairo. It is of a fine quality, almost white in colour, and in excellent condition; the handwriting is also very clear and bold. It records a certain official examination consequent on injuries or thefts perpetrated in the tombs or chapels of ten monarchs of the XIth, XIIIth and XVIIIth dynasties. Out of these ten royal tombs nine were found uninjured; the tenth, belonging to a monarch of the XIIIth dynasty, was found broken into and looted. The result of the examination of this tomb is recorded in full by the scribe and is given here :—

TRANSCRIPTION.

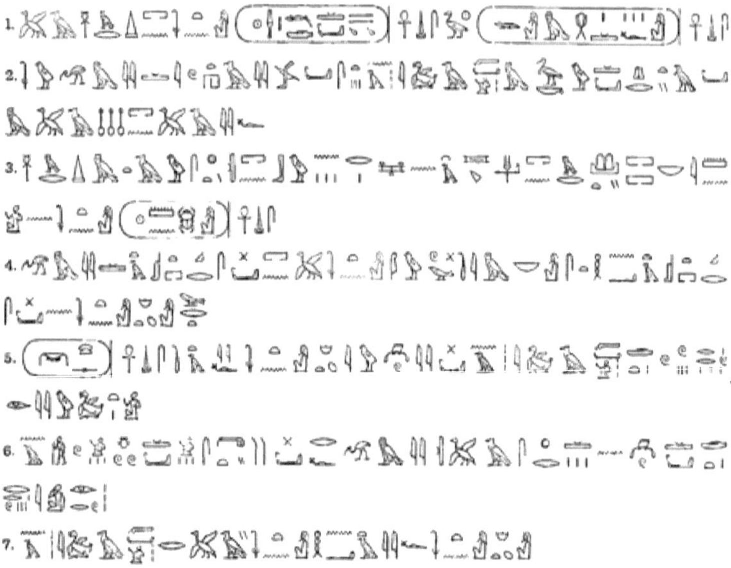

Transliteration.

1. *pa mer ne seten (Rá-sekhem-shed-taui)| ánkh uza senb sa Rá (Sebek-em-sau-ef)| ánkh uza senb.*
2. *su gemy án tehay set na ázan em baku kherti em pa neferu ne payef*
3. *mer em ta usekht ne ba-nu-re ne ta áa-mer ábá ne mer shenuti Neb-Ámen ne seten (Rá-men-kheper)| ánkh uza senb*
4. *gemy ta ást kres ne pa seten shutám neb set hená ta ást kres ne hemt seten urt*
5. *(Nub-khá-es)| ánkh uza senb tayef hemt seten áu fny na ázau det reru áryu zat*
6. *na seru ubau semeti ref gemy pa sekher ne fu det reru á áru*
7. *na ázu er pui seten hená tayef hemt seten.*

Translation.

1. "The tomb of king Ra-sekhem-shed-taui, L.P.H! son of Ra, Sebek-em-sau-ef L.P.H!
2. "It was found that the thieves had entered it by undermining the principal chamber of the
3. "monument from the outer chamber of the tomb of the superintendent of the granaries Neb-Amen of king Ra-men-kheper [Thothmes III] L.P.H.!
4. "The grave of the king was found to be without its lord; so also was the grave of the great royal wife
5. "Nub-kha-es, his royal spouse; the thieves had laid hands on them.
6. "The vezir, the nobles and stewards investigated the matter and found the thieves having laid hands on them, a fact,
7. "as far as the king and his royal wife were concerned."

Such is the official account given of the examination of the tomb. From the Amherst Papyrus No. VI it appears that there were eight thieves concerned, and they were nearly all servants of the temple of Amen. It will be observed also, as Prof. Erman has pointed out, that a stone-cutter was amongst the number, and perhaps it was he who had made the underground passage to the tomb described in the Abbott Papyrus. The record of their trial and confession is of extreme interest, and is given in full in the Amherst document. Having been, as was the custom for suspects, beaten on their hands and feet with sticks, they confessed that they had made their way into the tomb and found the bodies of the king and queen there. Their confession runs:—

["The tomb of the king Sebekemsauf and] of the royal wife Nub-khā-es his wife. The tomb was surrounded by masonry closed up with stones and covered over with *khesh-khesh*. This we broke through and found in it the royal mummies. We opened their coffins and the wrappings which were on them, and we found many amulets and necklaces of gold. The head of the king was covered with gold and the mummy was adorned with gold throughout.

"The wrappings were of gold and silver within and without, and covered with every kind of precious stone. We tore off the gold that we found, together with all the amulets and necklaces which were on his neck and the wrappings on which they lay.

"We found the mummy of the royal wife also, and we took all that which we found from it, and we set fire to their wrappings and we took all their funerary furniture consisting of vessels of gold, silver and copper. We divided all this into eight pieces [among our eight selves]."

Of the eight thieves, the names of five are preserved. These were, with one exception, all servants of officials of the temple of Amen. By trade one, as before mentioned, was a stone-cutter, another was a labourer in the service of an overseer of the huntsmen, the third was a husbandman from Karnak, the fourth a water-carrier of the Kenau of king Thothmes IV, and the fifth a soldier (?).

The public confession was not enough; the thieves were also obliged to identify the scene of their crime. "On the 19th day of the 3rd month of the summer season of the 16th year" (of Ramses IXth's reign), runs the text, "the thieves were taken before the governor and wazir Kha-em-uas and his lieutenant, and in their presence they were ordered to identify the tomb" to which their confession referred. Their guilt being finally established, the wazir and his officer sent in their official report to the king, for it seems that a law forbade the governor and his court to pass sentence upon tomb violators. The criminals were meanwhile handed over to the high priest of Amen to be confined in the prison temple "with their fellow thieves." The sentence passed upon them is not recorded, but we can well believe that, like other miscreants of the period, they were condemned to death, probably by the most ignominious punishment then known—death by their own hand.

Another important trial of robbers took place in the seventeenth year of Ramses IXth's reign, and the court consisted of the same wazir and officers. This was a case of robbery of gold, silver and copper at Thebes. It is recorded in the Papyrus Harris A, tracings of which are now preserved at Didlington Hall.* Dated in the "17th year, the 1st month of the spring season, the day 5," it gives a list of the names of the thieves, whose trade, occupation or profession is in every instance noted. The court of the wazir consisted of the governor himself Kha-em-uas, the high priest of Amen, Amen-

* These tracings preserve some 41 lines which are not now to be found in the document in the British Museum.

hetep, the prince Paser,* the chief scribe of the auditors Un-nefer, and the chief foreman User-Khepesh. The wazir Kha-em-uas is, as we have seen, mentioned in several other documents. The prince Paser appears in the great trial recorded in the Abbott Papyrus, and the name of the foreman User-Khepesh in other documents preserved in the British Museum, at Liverpool and in Turin.

Among the prisoners were merchants, scribes, weavers, metal workers and other artificers, guards, peasants, water-carriers, bakers and oil-boilers, slaves, washermen, canal-workers, a barber, several seamstresses and other Theban women, a gardener and a captain of Nubian soldiers. Most of these people were inhabitants of eastern Thebes, and were employed in the service of the high priest of Amen or served in the temple of Amen. Others belonged to the temple buildings of the kings, such as to the *Kenau* or to the temple of Amenhetep III, or to the temples of Thothmes I, of Seti I or Ramses III. Several held posts in the royal granary or granaries of the temple of Amen or of Khonsu. Many of the criminals lived in the necropolis on the western bank of the river. Several were from the Fayum; others were attached to the service of the god Sebek of Atur in the Fayûm, of Khnum of Elephantine, and of Mentu of Erment.

IV.

The VIIIth papyrus of the Amherst Collection belongs to a great treatise on the Geography of Egypt and the Fayûm written in the Ptolemaic period, perhaps under Ptolemy Euergetes II. It is doubtful however whether it originally formed part of the roll of the great Fayûm papyrus, portions of which are preserved in the Gizeh Museum, in Austria and in England, or whether it formed another volume of the same book. The latter supposition would seem most probable, for the scattered parts from Gizeh, Vienna and Lincoln have recently been fitted together by M. Lanzoni of Turin, and the document appears to present no gaps. The Amherst Papyrus No. VIII however is of the same date, and is written in the same handwriting. It enumerates the various names or provinces of Egypt in their geographical order, and gives a figure of the crocodile-god Sebek, as the local divinity of each. It also gives a representation of the temple and acacia tree of Neith, which it is stated was situated "at the side of" the temple of Sebek, Lord of Ri-seh.

V.

Of the miscellaneous papyri but three call for special notice. No. IX, of which unfortunately only part of the first two pages and the last lines of three others remain, related to the legend of the goddess Astarte. Had it been complete it would perhaps have been the most valuable document of the whole collection. But little can now be rescued from it. It mentions Astarte as the "little one of Ptah," and the early part referred to some god or other person who bore the tribute of the sea. This tribute is further stated to have consisted of silver, gold, lapis lazuli and wood.

Papyrus No. X, of which only two fragments remain, is written in the beautiful hieratic writing characteristic of the middle kingdom. The smaller fragment names a certain Sebek-hetep; the larger mentions domestic animals, flax, beads. It probably formed part of some official account-book like the Great Account Papyrus of the Gizeh Museum (*Boulac Papyrus*, No. 18).

* Lord Amherst possesses the lower part of an *ushabti* figure inscribed with this prince's name.

The two fragments of Papyrus No. XI belong to the series of accounts of the time of Seti I preserved in the Museum of the Louvre, and published by Dr. Spiegelberg in his *Rechnungen aus der Zeit Seti I.*

VI.

The series of Books of the Dead preserved at Didlington Hall represents copies of various chapters written for twenty-four individuals, several of whom bore titles of high rank. Among them occur one for a guard of the treasury, another for a chief librarian of the king, a third for a superintendent of the royal granaries. Several name musicians attached to the service of the temple of Amen. Others were written for priests of Amen-Ra, Ra, Khonsu and other deities. They were probably all found in the necropolis of Thebes, but the origin of one of them is alone certain. This is Papyrus No. XXXV, the first half of which is now preserved in the British Museum. This latter part was purchased from the Salt Collection, and is stated to have come from Thebes. It measures eighteen inches wide and about sixteen feet in length. It is one of the finest hieratic copies of the Book of the Dead in existence.

List of the Chapters of the Book of the Dead, of which complete copies, or parts of copies, are preserved among the Amherst Papyri.*

CHAPTER

I in Papyri Nos. XVI, XVII, XXXVI, XXXVIII.

VII ,, ,, XXXIV, XXXVI.

VIII in Papyrus No. XXXI.

IX ,, ,, XXXIV.

XI in Papyri Nos. XXII, XXXVI.

XII ,, ,, XXII, XXXIV.

* I have adopted the system of numbering the chapters employed by Lepsius in his edition of the *Todtenbuch*. This is also the system employed by Naville and Budge.

CHAPTER

XIII in Papyrus No. XXII.

XV in Papyri Nos. XXIII, XXIV, XXXIV, XXXVI.

XVI in Papyrus No. XXXVI.

XVII ,, ,, XVII.

XVIII in Papyri Nos. XXIV, XXVIII, XXXVI.

XXVII in Papyrus No. XXXIV.

XXVIII ,, ,, XXXIV.

XXXII ,, ,, XXV.

XXXIII ,, ,, XXV.

XXXVII ,, ,, XXII.

XXXVIII ,, ,, XXII.

XLI in Papyri Nos. XXII, XXV.

XLII ,, ,, XVI, XXV

XLVI in Papyrus No. XXXI.

XLVIII ,, ,, XVIII.

LI ,, ,, XVIII.

LIV ,, ,, XVI.

LVII ,, ,, XVI.

LVIII ,, ,, XVI.

LXI ,, ,, XVI.

LXIII in Papyri Nos. XVI, XXV.

LXVII in Papyrus No. XVI.

LXXV ,, ,, XVI.

LXXVI ,, ,, XVIII.

LXXVII in Papyri Nos. XXV, XXVII.

LXXIX in Papyrus No. XXII.

LXXXII in Papyri Nos. XVIII, XXV.

LXXXV in Papyrus No. XXV.

LXXXVI ,, ,, XXV.

LXXXVII in Papyri Nos. XVIII, XXV.

LXXXVIII in Papyrus No. XXV.

LXXXIX in Papyri Nos. XXIII, XXV.

XCI ,, ,, XVII, XXII.

XCII ,, ,, XVII, XXII.

XCIII ,, ,, XVII, XXII.

XCIV in Papyrus No. XXII.

XCVIII ,, ,, XXV.

XCIX in Papyri Nos. XVI, XXV.

CV ,, ,, XVI, XVII, XXV.

CVIII in Papyrus No. XXII.

CIX ,, ,, XXII.

CX in Papyri Nos. XVII, XXX, XXXII, XXXV.

CXI in Papyrus No. XXXV.

CXIII ,, ,, XXXV.

CXIV ,, ,, XXXV.

CXV ,, ,, XXXV.

CXVII ,, ,, XXXV.

CXVIII ,, ,, XXXV.

CXIX ,, ,, XXXV.

CXX ,, ,, XXXV.

CXXI in Papyri Nos. XVII, XXV, XXXV.

CXXII in Papyrus No. XXXV.

CHAPTER
CXXIV in Papyrus No. XVII.
CXXV in Papyri Nos. XVI, XVII, XXI, XXXIV, XXXV.
CXXVI in Papyrus No. XXXV.
CXXVII " " XVI.
CXXVIII " " XXXV.
CXXIX " " XXXV.
CXXXII " " XXXV.
CXXXV " " XXXV.
CXXXVI " " XVII.
CXXXVII in Papyri Nos. XVI, XVII, XXXV.
CXXXVIII in Papyrus No. XXXV.
CXLI " " XVIII.
CXLIV in Papyri Nos. XVI, XVII.
CXLV " " XVI, XVII, XXII, XXXIV.
CXLVI " " XIX, XXXIV.

CHAPTER
CXLVIII in Papyri Nos. XXXIV, XXXV.
CXLIX " " XVI, XX, XXXIV.
CL in Papyrus No. XXXIV.
CLI " " XXXIV.
CLII in Papyri Nos. XVI, XXXIV, XXXV.
CLIV " " XXXIV, XXXV.
CLV in Papyrus No. XXXV.
CLVII in Papyri Nos. XXXIV, XXXV.
CLVIII in Papyrus No. XXXV.
CLIX in Papyri Nos. XXXIV, XXXV.
CLIX bis in Papyrus No. XXXV.
CLXI in Papyri Nos. XXXIV, XXXV.
CLXII in Papyrus No. XXXIV.
CLXIII " " XXXIV.
CLXIV " " XXXIV.
CLXV in Papyri Nos. XXII, XXXIV.

HIEROGLYPHIC AND HIERATIC PAPYRI.

A. EARLY LITERARY FRAGMENTS.

PAPYRUS No. I.

(Plate I. A–E.)

Five fragments written in the bold hieratic writing characteristic of the Middle Kingdom. They originally formed part of the outer roll of a great papyrus said to have been found at Thebes and now preserved in the Berlin Museum (Papyrus No. 3023, published in L.D. vi, 108–110). The fragments measure in height and width respectively:—A. 6 inches by 3½ inches. B. 5 inches by 2 inches. C. 5¼ inches by 3¼ inches. D. 1¾ inches by 1½ inches. E. 2¾ inches by 2 inches.

Transcription.

In the following transcription the restorations have been made from the parallel text of the Butler Papyrus in the British Museum. From that text it appears that the first two lines of the tale are destroyed in the Amherst copy. The ends of the third to the tenth horizontal lines are preserved, but as they only give various determinatives for the names of products of the Sekhet Hemat, they are not given in the transcription. Lines 11–14 are destroyed; the text therefore begins with l. 15:—

Fragment A. Fragment B. Fragment C. Fragments D and E.

C

Transliteration.

15. *em ánu neb nefer ne Sekhet-Ḥemat*
16. *[shemt] pu ár ne Sekhti pen em khent-*
17. *[yt] er Ḥenen-seten, sper pu ár nef er u ne per*
18. *Fefá, ḥer meḥti em dená, gem nef se ám áḥá*
19. *ḥer mery[t], Ḥemti ren ef, sa [se pu Ásry]*
20. *ren ef, zet pu net mer per ur Merui-ten[sa zed án]*
21. *Ḥemti pen maa ef áa ne Sekhti pen*
22. *áabyu ḥer áb ef, zed ef. ḥa [ná shepa neb]*
23. *[men]kh áua [ḥenu ne Sekhti pen]*
24. *ám ef! ást ref ár per Ḥemti pen ḥer sema-ta [ne re ne]*
25. *uat ḥens pu, nen usekh, ás pu qen[ef]*
26. *er sekhu ne ry, áu uat ef uát kher mu [ket]*
27. *[y]ef uat ef resi zed án Ḥemti pen [ne shemsu ef]*
28. *[ás! án-ná áfd em perui; án ám-ef ḥer-á;]*
29. *[áḥá ne seshem nef pa áfd ḥer p]a sema-ta ne re uat*
30. *un án khenen [sedeb ef ḥer] mu nepnept [ef]*
31. *[ḥer] resi. áu án [ref Sekhti pen] ḥer uat net rekh [32 neb].*

Translation.

15. With all the good products of the Sekhet-Hemat.
16. The said Sekhti [journeyed] southwards
17. to Henen-seten and when he came to the land belonging to the house of
18. Fefa on the north of the dyke he found a man there standing
19. upon the bank, whose name was the Hemti son [of a man named Asry]
20. a serf of the chief steward Meruiten[sa. Said]
21. this Hemti when he saw the asses of [this] Sekhti
22. which pleased him, said he, "May [every excellent image (of a god)]
23. rob the [goods of the Sekhti]
24. from him!" Now the Hemti's house was at the bank [of the tow]
25. path (?) which was narrow, but not broad; it would amount
26. to the width of a girdle; one edge of the road had water, the [other]
27. side had corn. Said the Hemti [to his servant
28. "Hasten! bring me a square chest from the house;" it was brought thence
29. immediately; then he opened the chest at] the bank of the tow path (?)
30. and it rested with [its cover on] the water and [its] *nepnept*
31. [on] the corn.

Now [the Sekhti] came along the path used by all men . . . ."

PAPYRUS No. II.

(Plate I. F. G.)

Two fragments of a second text of the Story of the Peasant which do not appear to belong to either of the Berlin copies. The writing upon them is hieratic of the Middle Kingdom, and somewhat like the hand of Papyrus No. I. They are probably from the Lieder Collection.

PAPYRUS No. III.

(Plate I. H–L.)

Four fragments written in a similar handwriting to Papyri Nos. I and II. They perhaps belong to a literary work now destroyed; the largest fragment only measures 2¾ inches high by 2 inches in width.

PAPYRUS No. IV.

(Plate I. M–Q.)

Five fragments originally forming part of the outer roll of Papyrus No. I of the Berlin Museum, and containing parts of the first lines of the celebrated Story of Sanehat. The writing is hieratic of the Middle Kingdom. They were probably obtained together with Papyri Nos. I, II and III. The fragments measure in height and width respectively:—M, 1¾ inches by 1 inch. N, 2¼ inches by 3 inches. O, 1 inch by ¼ inch. P, 5 inches by 1¾ inches. Q, 1½ inches by 1 inch.

It would have been impossible to identify these fragments as belonging to the Berlin Papyrus No. I, had no other copy of the tale existed. Prof. Maspero was fortunate enough to discover in 1881, in a tomb at Thebes, a late hieratic ostracon (XXth dynasty), which on examination was found to contain a copy of the beginning of the Sanehat story. The text was afterwards published by Maspero and, although it is very corrupt, it enables us to ascertain the exact position of the Amherst fragments. Numbering backwards from the beginning of the Berlin Papyrus, the lines in the Amherst fragments may be designated as 16, 15; 12, 11, 10, 9, 8; 4, 3, 2, 1; the last almost joins the Berlin manuscript.

In the first fragment (Plate I, M) the hieratic signs are too mutilated to be decipherable; but in l. 15 there are the signs 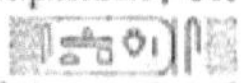 belonging to the cartouche of Amenemhat I 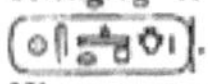. In the second fragment (lettered N) are parts of five lines (ll. 12–8).

The third fragment (lettered O) contains only three signs; on the fourth and fifth (lettered P. Q) are remains of four lines.

4. 

3. 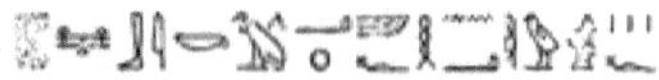

2. is too mutilated to decipher.

1. 

By the help of these fragments and Prof. Maspero's late ostracon, an attempt to reconstruct the text in the style of the ancient papyrus has been made by Mr. F. Ll. Griffith. It is to be found in the *Proceedings of the Society of Biblical Archæology*, Vol. XIV, p. 452.

B. LEGAL PAPYRI.

PAPYRUS No. V. (The Lee Papyrus.)

(*Vide* Plates II and III.)

Fragments of two pages of a papyrus containing an abstract of criminal proceedings dealing with a case of sorcery, written in a beautiful hieratic handwriting of the XXth dynasty (*circa* Ramses III).

This papyrus was bought by Dr. Lee at Mr. Burton's sale (*Hartwell House Catalogue*, No. 436), and purchased by Lord Amherst of Hackney with Dr. Lee's Egyptian collection about 1868. The fragments were then mounted and arranged as in Dr. Lee's fac-simile (*l.c.* Pl. II), but were placed in their right order in 1892 by the present writer. The document was first fac-similed by S. Sharpe (*Egyptian Inscriptions*, Second Series, Pls. LXXXVII–VIII) in 1855, and three years later Dr. Lee gave a lithographic reproduction of it in his *Hartwell House Catalogue* (Pl. II). In 1860, Chabas published a transcription and study of the text in his essay on *Le Papyrus Magique Harris* (pp. 169–173), and in 1865, T. Deveria gave an account of it in the *Journal Asiatique*, No. 9, with a reproduction of Sharpe's fac-simile.* A short notice has also been given of it by Prof. Erman (*Zeitschrift für Aegyptische sprache*, 1879, pp. 76 ff.), and by Dr. Spiegelberg in his valuable essay on Egyptian law (*Studien und Materialien zum Rechtswesen des Pharaonenreiches der Dynast XVIII–XXI*, p. 132).

The papyrus consists of two pages measuring respectively: 1st page, 19 inches long by 9½ inches high; 2nd page, 11 inches long by 9½ inches high.

* Reprinted in Maspero's *Bibliothèque Égyptologique*, Tome 5, Plates IX and X.

TRANSCRIPTION.

Page 1.

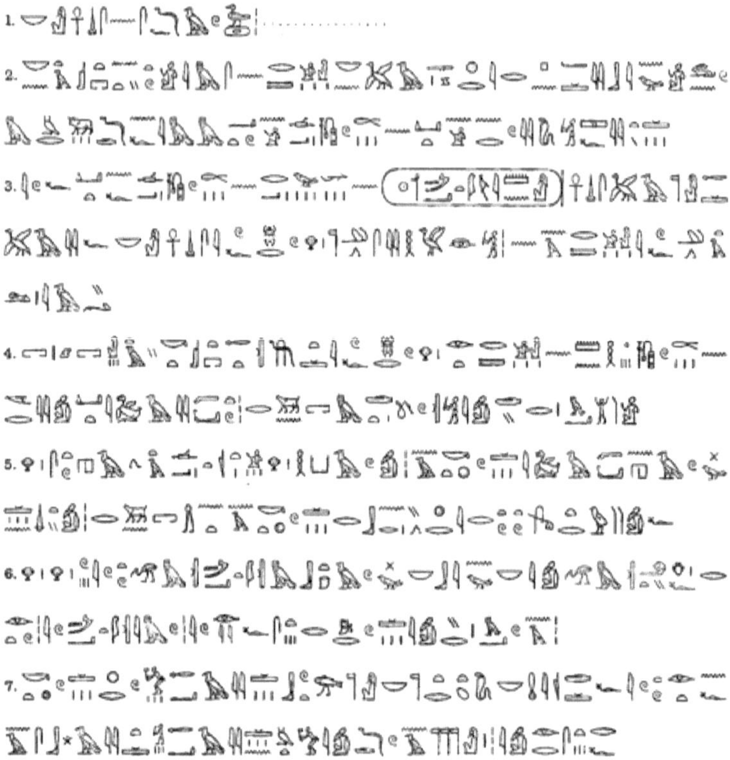

Transliteration.

I.

1. *neb ānkh uza senb ne se-zefuu . . . . . . [reth]*
2. *neb ne ta āst netī tuā ām sen reth neb ne pa ta kher ār Pen-ḥuy-bān unn em mer āḥu zed nef āmmātu nā uī seshu ne dut nā neruy shefyt*
3. *āuf dut nef uā seshu ne rā ne (Rā-user-maāt mery-Amen) ānkh uza senb pa neter aā payf neb ānkh uza senb āuf kheperu ḥer neter peḥ syḥ ne na reth āuf peḥ ta lāāuī [ne]*
4. *per khen tai ket āst aāt zat āuf kheperu ḥer ārt reth ne menḥ seshu ne mery dut āzaytu er khen em det rudu Adī-ra-mā*
5. *ḥer setu ha ta uat ḥedet ḥer ḥekau na ketekhu āza neḥau ne medetī er khen ānt na ketekhu er ben-ri kher ār tutu se-meteruf*
6. *ḥer ḥeru āu tu gem maāt em betau neb bān neb ā gem ḥatī ef er ārtu āu maāt āmu āu āry-ef set er zeru ā-ī-rī-māu na*
7. *ketekhu kheru āay but neter neb netert neb ma ḥed-ef au tu ārt nef na sebayt āay ne met ā zedu na neteru ā ār set ref*

Translation.

I.

1. The Lord L.P.H. for the provisioning . . . .
2. All [people] of the place in which I am and all people of the land. Now Penhuiban being superintendent of the cattle said to him: "Bring me a book which will tell me how to perform feats of cunning and strength."
3. Then he gave to him a book of magical receipts from the library (?) of Ra-user-maat Mery Amen (Ramses III) L.P.H. the great god his lord L.P.H. whereby he could strike blind the people and reach the innermost recesses
4. of the harem and other secret places. [By one of its receipts] he made figures of wax and love charms and these he had carried to the interior in the hand of an officer named Adi-ra-mā.
5. So that one of the workmen might be removed and the others bewitched and that thereby certain words might be taken to the interior chamber and bring others to the outside. Now they were examining him about it
6. it was found to be true and all that he had done in his heart was abominable and bad. The truth of it was that he made these things together with
7. the other great criminals whom all and every god and goddess abominate. They pronounced upon him the great judgment of death decreed by the gods.

TRANSCRIPTION

Page 2.

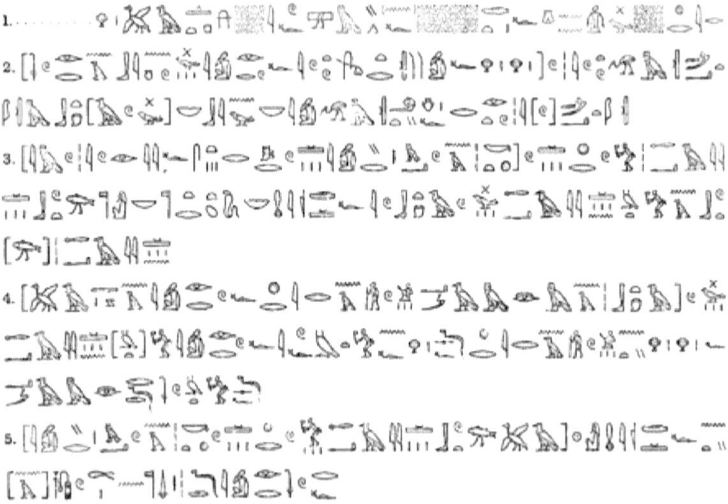

Transliteration.

1. . . . . *ḥer pa ḥetep . . . . ȧuf shemi nef . . . . det ef genen . . . . kher ȧr.*
2. *[su ȧr na binu ȧ ȧru f ȧn tu semeter-ef ḥer ḥer] u ȧn tu ḡem maat em bet [au] neb bȧu neb ȧ ḡem ḥati ef er ȧrtu ȧ[u] maat*
3. *[ȧmu ȧn ȧry-ef set er zeru ȧ-i-ri-mȧu na ketekh]u kheru ȧay but neter neb netert neb mȧ ḥed-ef au betau ȧay ne met au but ȧay ne*
4. *[pa ta na ȧ aru ef kher ȧr na seru ȧmam em na beta]u ȧay ne [met] ȧ ȧru ef ȧuf met ḥer zesef kher ȧr na seru neti ḥer ḥer ef ȧmam er zed su met zesef*
5. *[ȧ-i-ri-mȧu na ketekhu kheru ȧay but pu] Rā mȧ ḥedet ef neti [nu] seshu ne neter medu zed ȧ ȧr su ref.*

Translation.

1. . . . . upon the table . . . . he came to him . . . . his hand was paralysed . . . . Now
2. [he had done the evil thing. They examined him upon it] and it was found true in every abomination and every evil that their hearts desired to do. The truth
3. [of it was that he did these things in combination with the other] great criminals whom all gods and all goddesses hate entirely. These were the great crimes worthy of death, the great abomination of
4. [the land. They stated that the great crimes were worthy of death which he did and he killed himself. Now the judges which were upon it saw that he killed himself.
5. With the other great criminals hated of Ra entirely, the books of the gods say "do thou it against [him]."

PAPYRUS No. VI. (The Amherst Papyrus.)

(*Vide* Plates IV–VII.)

The lower parts of three pages, and fragments of one other, of a papyrus containing the confession of a thief who had robbed the tomb of king [Sebek-em-sau-ef] and of his consort Nub-Khâs; also the names of other thieves implicated in the same robbery. It is written in a fairly good hieratic hand, but on the last page the hieratic becomes exceedingly cursive and somewhat resembles that of the *verso* of the Abbott papyrus in the British Museum. The trial, of which the documents give an account, took place on "the 19th day of the 3rd month of the summer season" in the 16th year of a king whose name is not recorded. This monarch, however, must have been Ramses IX; it was his wazir and officers who tried the case.

The papyrus has been published in fac-simile by Chabas (*Mélanges Égyptologiques*, Troisième Série, Tome II, plates I–IV, pp. 1–26, together with a study of the text by himself and Dr. Birch. Prof. Erman has also written an essay upon it and other documents connected with the same case, in the *Zeitschrift für Aegyptische Sprache*, 1879, pp. 81, 148; *cf.* also the same author's *Aegypten*, pp. 189–198.

Page 1. (Plate IV.)

The fragments of the first page apparently give a list of names of persons implicated in the trial. In the plate the original spacing has been adhered to as far as possible.

TRANSCRIPTION. Page I (Plate IV).

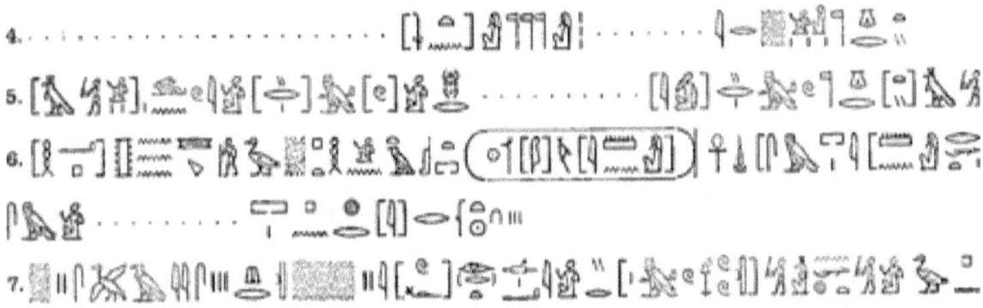

[Top of page II. 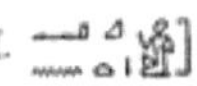]

Transliteration.

4. . . . . [*seten*] *neteru* . . . . *àr* . . . . *neter* *kherti*
5. *Unn à-* [*iry*] *md*[*u*] *kheper* . . . . . [*à*] *iry-mâu neter* *kherti*

6. *Hâpu sa Ptaḥ ne ta àst* (*Râ-user-*[*maâ*] *mery* [*Àmen*])| *ànkh uza* [*senb em per À*]*men er khet sem* . . . . *per pen kher* [*à*]*r renpit XIII.*

7. . . . *II s pays III kher* . . . . *II à* [*uf*] *àrt uà à-iry mâu ḥemuu Set-nekht sa Pen*[*-ànket*]

Translation.

Of the first five lines only a word here and there is preserved. At the end of line 5 is the title of "the necropolis worker," whose name is given in

Line 6. Hapu son of . . . . Ptah of the temple of Ramses III L.P.[H. in the house of] Amen, under the authority of the *Sem*-priest [. . . . . . . of] this house in the year XIII.

Line 7 mentions the "labourer" Set-nekht, son of Pen-[anket]. Set-nekht is again mentioned on page IV, l. 4.

TRANSCRIPTION. PAGE 2 (PLATE V).

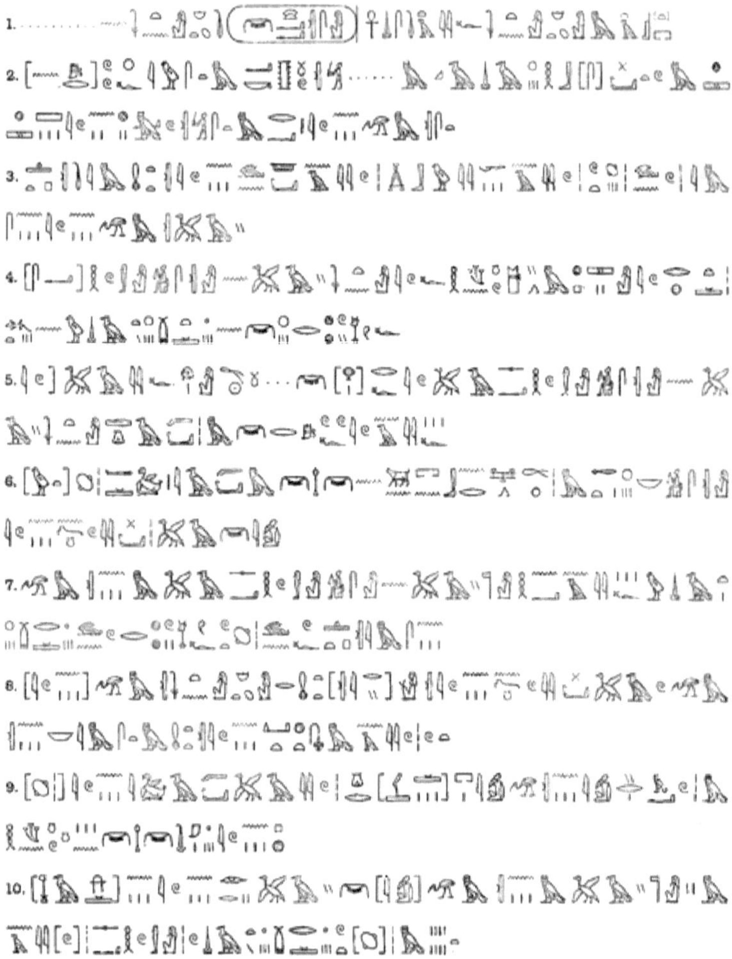

Trans-literation.

II.

1. . . . . . *ne seten ḥemt (Nub-khāā-es)| a.u.s. tay ef seten ḥemt em ta àst*
2. *[ne zer]uu khefàu-set mak ànb . . . . em ḥasa ḥe[b]s tu em khesh-khesh àu ne sep mau set em-rā àu nu gemi set*
3. *ḥetep thàm màtet àu ne un nayu àdebuy nayu ut unu àm sen àu ne gem paī*
4. *[sā] ḥu sheps ne paī seten àu f ḥenu em khepesh II àu rekhet àshert ne usat ne nub er khekhui ef*
5. *[àu] pay ef tep . . . . . . nub [ḥer] ref àu pa sāḥu sheps ne paī seten dega em nub er zeruu ef àu nay-f*
6. *[ut] ḥu za àu em nub ḥez nub ne khen ne ben-ri em aàt neb sheps àu nu nay pa nub à*
7. *gem nu em pa sāḥu sheps ne paī neter ḥenà nay ef usat àper unu er khekhuī ef ut unu ef ḥetep àm sen*
8. *[àu nu] gem seten ḥemt er màtet àrī àu nu nay pau gem nu neb àm set em màtet àu nu det khet em nayu ut*
9. *àu nu àza payu gerg per à gem nu à-l-ri-mà em ḥenu ne nub ḥez nub àu nu pekh*
10. *kha nu àu nu àr paī nub à gem nu em paī neter II em nay[u] sāḥu usat àper ut em VIII.*

Translation.

II.

1. . . . . . . of the royal wife Nub-khaa-es L.P.H., his royal wife in the place
2. it was surrounded by masonry, closed up with stones, protected by rubble, covered with slabs, but we penetrated them notwithstanding, and covered over with *khesh-khesh*, and we demolished it with work, and we found it
3. resting likewise. We opened their coffins and their wrappings which were in them and we found this
4. noble mummy of this king. It was found; there were two swords and things many of amulets and necklaces of gold on his neck,
5. his head was covered with gold upon it. The noble mummy of this king was adorned with gold throughout. Its wrappings were graven with gold and silver within and without and covered with every precious stone. We tore off the gold that
7. we found on the noble mummy of this god, together with his amulets and necklaces which were on his neck and the wrappings on which they rested.
8. We found the royal wife likewise. We tore off all that which we found from it likewise and we set fire to their
9. wrappings. We took their furniture which we found with them [consisting of], gold and silver and copper vases and
10. We divided and we made this gold which we found upon these two gods on their noble mummies and the amulets and the necklaces and the wrappings into 8 pieces.

TRANSCRIPTION.

Page 3 (Plate VI).

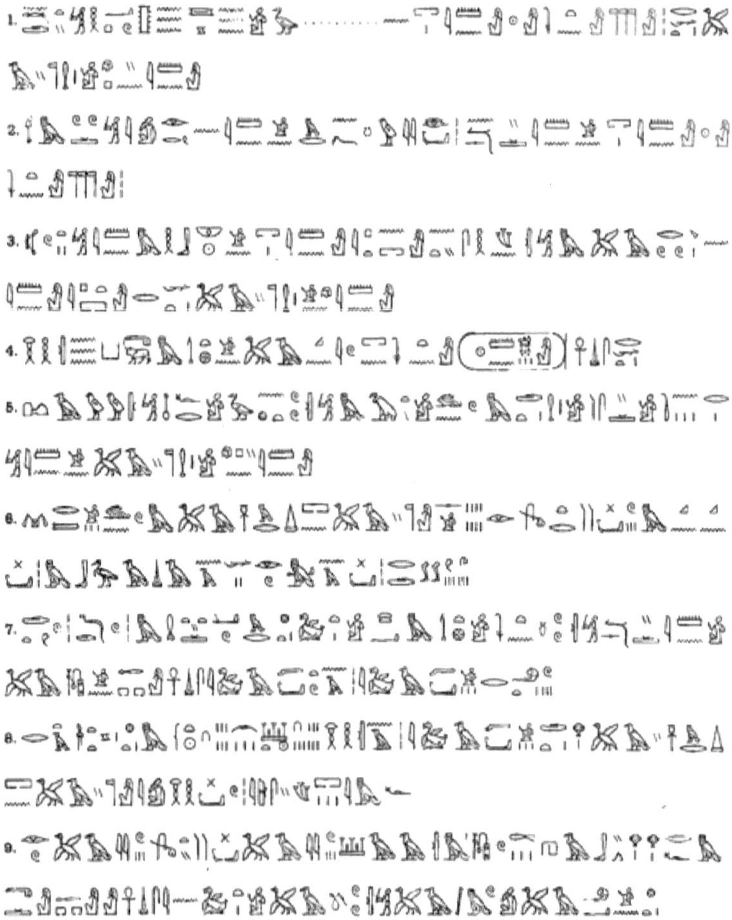

Transliteration.

III.

1. *neshedetī Hāpu sa . . . . . ne per Āmen-Rā seten neteru er khet paī neter ḥen tepī ne Āmen.*

2. *ḥemtuu Ā-ār-rī-ne-Āmen ne mer nuy Nesī-Āmen ne per Āmen-Rā seten neteru.*

3. *āhutī Āmen-em-ḥeb ne per Āmen-āpt netī seḥenu em pa rau ne Āmen-āpt er khet paī neter ḥen tep ne Āmen*

4. *uahī Ka-em-uast ne pa ḥenān ne per seten (Ra-men-kheperu) ānkh uza senb er khet*

5. *aḥauu Nefer sa Nekhtuu-em-Mat unu em det ḥen neḥesī Theun-rī-Āmen ne paī neter ḥen tepī ne Āmen.*

6. *demd reth unu em pa mer ne paī neter se VIII ār semeteru em ḥen-ḥen em ba-za-na āru māna redu*

7. *deta zedu em mātet du mer nut zat Khā-em-uast seten reduuī Nesī-Āmen pa sesh ne perui aā ānkh uza senb āzutu nau aza er ḥatu*

8. *er ta āmentet nut em renpet XVI ābd III shāt ḥeru XIX uaḥ na azu det her paī mer ne paī neter ā uaḥu āsī ām ef*

9. *āru payu semeterī payu shāau em seshu habī her ḥer ref em baḥ perui aā ānkh uza senb ān zat pa redun pa uḥemu pa ḥā ne nut.*

Translation.

III.

1. The stone-cutter Hapu, son of . . . . . of the house of Amen-Ra, king of the gods, and under the authority of the high priest of Amen.
2. The labourer A-ar-ri-en-Amen, of the overseer of the huntsmen, Nesi-Amen, of the house of Amen-Ra, king of the gods.
3. The husbandman Amen-em-heb, of the house of Amen-apt administrating in the district of Amen-apt, under the authority of the high priest of Amen.
4. The water-carrier Ka-em-uast, of the *kenan* of the king Thothmes IV L.P.H., under the authority of . . . . .
5. The *āhati* Nefer, son of Nekhtu-em-Mut, being in the hand of the negro slave Theuu-ri-amen of the high priest of Amen.
6. Total of the persons who were in the tomb of this god, 8 men: they were examined with blows of the stick: they were beaten upon their feet
7. and hands. They said likewise, and were given over to the governor of the city and wazir Kha-em-uast, and the royal officer Nesi-amen, the scribe of Pharaoh L.P.H. They took the thieves before them
8. to the west of the city, in the 16th year the 3rd month of the summer season the day 15. The thieves put their hand upon this tomb of this god and [also] upon the *asi*-chambers in it.
9. A record was made of the trial in writing and sent before the Pharaoh L.P.H., by the wazir, the lieutenant, the reporter, and the prince of the city.

TRANSCRIPTION.

PAGE 4 (PLATE VII).

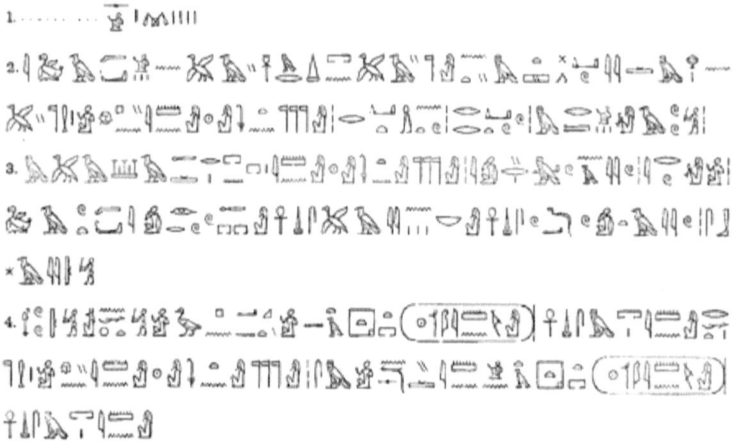

TRANSLITERATION.

1\. . . . . *se demd* IV

2\. *aza ne pai mer ne pai neter neti em tash duy em her ne pai neter hen tepi ne Ámen-Rā seten neteru er de ȧutu er erdetuu em reth zauu*

3\. *em pa sha aā ri ne per Ámen-Rā seten neteru ȧ-t-ri-mȧu mayu ȧru zaut ȧirwu perui ȧa ȧnkh uza senb pay nu neb ȧnkh uza senb uzȧu tayu sebay*

4\. *hemtuu Set-nekht sa Pen-ȧnket ne ta hat (Ra-user-maā mery Ámen)| ȧnkh uza senb em per Amen er khet neter hen tepi ne Ámen-Rā seten neteru sem Nesi-Ámen ne ta hat (Rā-user-maā mery Ámen)| ȧnkh uza senb em per Ámen.*

TRANSLATION.

1\. . . . . men: total, 4.

2\. Thieves of this tomb of this god who absconded and were given over to the high priest of Amen-Ra, king of the gods, in order to summon them

3\. and make them prisoners in the prison of the house of Amen, king of the gods, with their brother-thieves whose punishment the Pharaoh L.P.H., our Lord, shall decide.

4\. The labourer Set-nekht, son of Pen-anket, of the temple of Ramses III L.P.H., in the house of Amen and under the authority of the high priest of Amen-Ra, the king of the gods the *sem* priest Nesi-amen of the temple of Ramses III L.P.H., in the house of Amen.

PAPYRUS No. VII.

(*Vide* Plates VIII–XIV.)

Original tracings of a papyrus formerly belonging to Mr. Harris of Alexandria, and much damaged whilst in his possession, the last lines of the pages being almost entirely destroyed. The tracings were made by Miss Harris about the year 1860, when the document was in a perfect state, and preserve about forty lines of the original. The mutilated papyrus itself was found at Medinet Habu about 1860 and purchased by the Trustees of the British Museum in 1885: it is now in the National Collection. The tracings have been carefully compared with the papyrus and the extent of its damage can be at once seen on reference to the Plates VIII–XIV.

This once magnificent document is written in the large and bold hieratic writing (which is sometimes very cursive) of the end of the XXth dynasty. It is dated in the 17th year of the reign of Ramses IX and refers to a case of robbery of gold, silver, and copper stolen from tombs in the Theban necropolis.

In the 6th line of page 1 (Pl. VIII) it is stated that the case was tried by the wazir Kha-em-uast and the high priest of Amen, Amen-hetep. The names of over one hundred persons of various trades and occupations, implicated in the robbery, are given: many of them are known also from other papyri (*vide* Introduction, p. 13).

TRANSCRIPTION. Page 1 (Plate VIII).

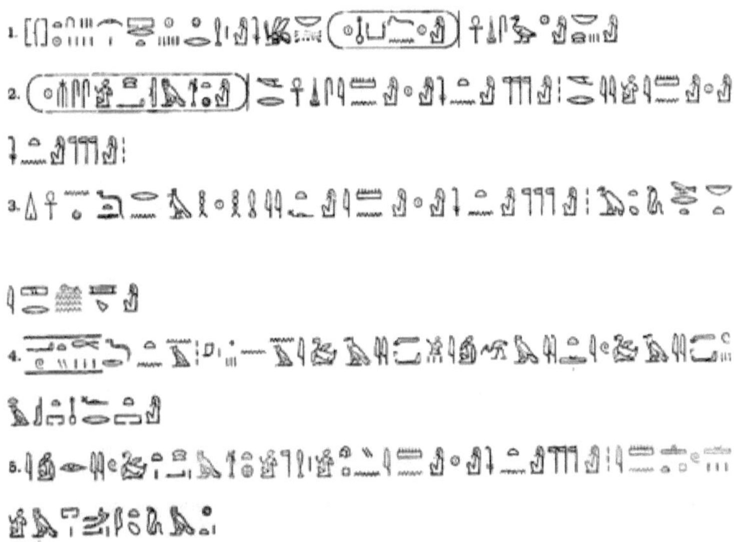

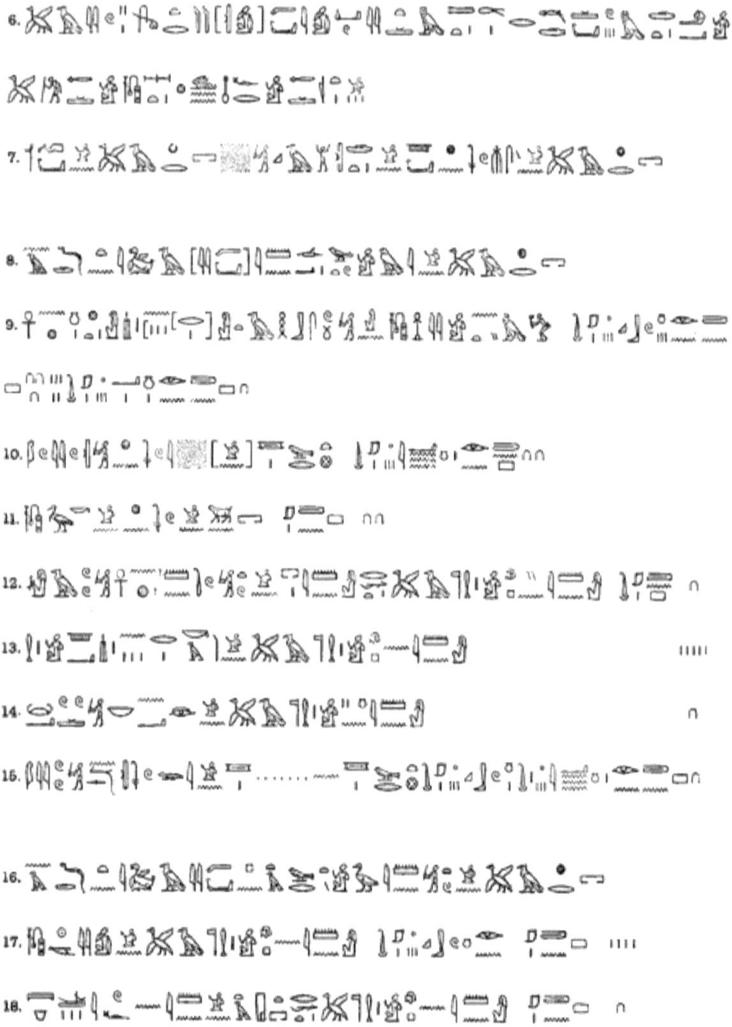

Transliteration.

I.

1. [Renpit] XVII ȧbd 1 pert ḥeru V kher ḥen seten bati neb taui (Rā-nefer-ka-setep-en-Rā)| A.U.S. sa Rā neb khāu

2. (Rā-meses khā-em-uast)| A.U.S. mery Ȧmen-Rā seten neteru mery Ȧmen-Rā seten neteru

3. ṭe ānkh zet er neḥeḥ mā ātef-ef Ȧmen-Rā seten neteru Mut uret nebt Ȧsheru

4. ȧuti zedet ne na nau ḥemt ne na āzay a yemyt ȧu zayu ta ȧst nefert

5. ȧ ȧryu zat Khā-em-uast neter ḥen tepi ne Ȧmen-Rā seten neteru Ȧmen-ḥetepu em per Maāt em uat

6. payu semeter ȧ duyt em thet er shed em det ḥa Paser-aā sesh ḥesept Un-nefer aā ḳedetu

7. User-khepesh ne pa kher .... ḳa-det ne ȧ Khensu-mes ne pa kher

8. na zedet ne azay Ȧmen-nā-shert Ḥerȧ ne pa kher

9. ānkh ne nut Ȧn-nu-[re] ta ḥeban ne sesh Seny enti em met ḥesmen ḳebu ȧr n deben 35 ḥesmen ȧ ȧr deben 10.

10. Khuyuu Khensu-ȧ ..... [ne] Mer-ur ḥesmen ȧȧ ȧr deben 20.

11. sesh Bāk-en-khensu ne kheun ḥemt deben 20.

12. sauu Ȧnkh (?)-Mentu-nekhtu ne per Ȧmen er khet pa neter ḥen tepi ne Ȧmen, ḥesment deben 10

13. ḥen Ȧ-ȧn-nu-reka ne pa neter ḥen tepi ne Ȧmen. 5

14. uḥānu Neb-nā ne pa neter ḥen sen ne Ȧmen. 10

15. shyuu Nes-su-sebek-ȧ ne mer ..... ne Mer-ur ḥesmen ḳebu ḥesmen ȧȧ ȧr deben 10

16. na zedet ne āzay Pen-ta-ur sa Ȧmen-nekhtu ne pa kher

17. sesh Ra-mery ne pa neter ḥen tepi ne Ȧmen ḥesmen ḳebu ȧr ḥemtu deben 4.

18. ḥer uekh Ȧuf-ne-Ȧmen ne ta ḥat er khet pa neter ḥen tepi ne Ȧmen, ḥemt deben 10.

Translation.

I.

1. [The year] 17, the first month of the spring season, the day 5, under the majesty of the king of Upper and Lower Egypt, Ra-nefer-ka-setep-en-Ra L.P.H., son of Ra, lord of the crowns,

2. Ramses [IX] shining in Thebes L.P.H., beloved of Amen-Ra, king of the gods, beloved of Amen-Ra, king of the gods (*sic*).

3. Giving life eternally for ever like his father Amen-Ra, king of the gods and Mut the great lady of Asher.

4. List of the names of the metal thieves who were found to have robbed the necropolis, and who were examined

5. by the wazir Kha-em-uast and the high priest of Amen-Ra king of the gods Amen-hetep in the house of Maat in the city (Thebes),

6. and (their names) were written down in order that they might be arrested by the prince Paser-aa the scribe of the nome, Un-nefer, the chief of the workmen

7. User-Khepesh of the necropolis .... ka-det of the doorkeeper Khonsu-mes of the necropolis

8. The statement of the thief Amen-na-shert and Hora of the necropolis.

9. The woman Au-nu-re, the seamstress of the scribe Seny who is dead. Bronze vessels making 35 deben, a ...... making 10 deben.

10. The merchant Khonsu-a ..... of the Fayum. Metal vases making 20 deben.

11. The scribe Bak-en-khonsu of the cabinet. Copper deben 20.

12. The guardian Ankh-(?) Menthu-nekhtu of the house of Amen under the authority of the high priest of Amen. Copper deben 10.

13. The slave A-an-nu-reka of the high priest of Amen. 5.

14. The boat-man Neb-na of the second priest of Amen. 10.

15. The merchant Nes-su-sebeka of Mer .... of the Fayum. Copper *kebu*-vessels copper *ȧȧ*-vessels making 10 deben.

16. The statement of the thief Pen-ta-ur son of Amennekht of the necropolis.

17. The scribe Ra-mery of the high priest of Amen. Copper vessels making copper 4 deben.

18. The boat-*reise* Auf-en-Amen of the temple and under the authority of the high priest of Amen. Copper 10 deben.

TRANSCRIPTION.

Page 2 (Plate IX).

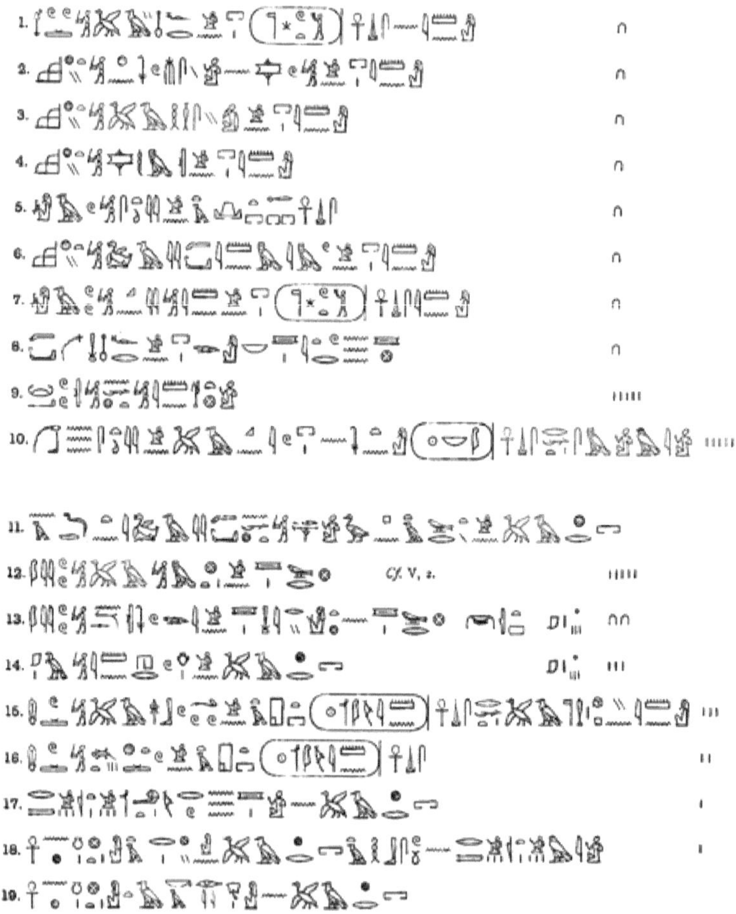

Transliteration.

II.

1. *ḥemtun Pai-nefer ne per (Neter-duat)*, *A.U.S. ne Ȧmen* 10.
2. *sekheti Khensu-mes ne nefuu ne per Ȧmen* 10.
3. *sekheti Pa-ḥesi ne per Ȧmen* 10.
4. *sekheti Nef-nezem ne per Ȧmen* 10.
5. *sau Sety ne ta shent perai aȧ A.U.S.* 10.
6. *sekheti zay Ȧmen-em-ȧmu ne per Ȧmen* 10.
7. *sau Ḳeny-Ȧmen ne per (Neter-duat) A.U.S. Ȧmen* 10.
8. ..... *Sen-nefer ne per Sebek neb mer ȧteru* 10.
9. *nḥuiu Nekht-Ȧmen-uast* 5.
10. *uāb Sety ne pa ḳemȧu ne seten (Ra-neb-maā)*, *A.U.S. er khet sem Ḥerȧ* 5.
11. *na zedet ne ȧzay Nekht-min sa Pen-ta-ur ne pa kher*
12. *shyuu Pa-nekht-em-nut ne Mer-ur* 5.
13. *shyuu Nes-su-sebek-ȧ ne Mer-sen-ȧrī ne Mer-ur nub ḳedet ḥemt* 20.
14. *ḥemti Ȧmen-heru-ȧb ne pa kher* *ḥemt* 3.
15. *debu Pa-ȧbu-nekht ne ta ḥat (Rā-user-maā mery Ȧmen)*, *A.U.S. er khet pa neter ḥen tepi ne Ȧmen* 3.
16. *debu Ȧshertu-khetu ne ta ḥat (Rā-user-maā mery Ȧmen)*, *A.U.S.* 2.
17. *reth ḳedet User-ḥāt-meru ne pa kher* 2.
18. *ȧnkh ne nut Ta-ry-sepi ne pa kher ta ḥebsu ne reth ḳedet Ḥerȧ* 1.
19. *ȧnkh ne nut Ta-ka-ȧry ne pa kher* 1.

Translation.

II.

1. The craftsman Pai-nefer, of the house of divine worship L.P.H., of Amon. 10.
2. The weaver Khonsu-mes, of the boatmen of the temple of Amen. 10.
3. The weaver Pa-hesi, of the temple of Amen. 10.
4. The weaver Nefu-nezem, of the temple of Amen. 10.
5. The guardian Sety, of the granary of Pharaoh L.P.H. 10.
6. The weaver and sculptor Amen-em-amu, of the temple of Amen. 10.
7. The guardian Keny-Amen, of the house of divine worship L.P.H., of Amen. 10.
8. The ...., Sen-nefer, of the temple of Sebek, lord of Mer-ateru. 10.
9. The boatman Nekht-amen-uast. 5.
10. The *uab*-priest Sety, of the *kemau* of the king Ra-neb-maā (Amenhetep III) L.P.H., under the authority of the *sem*-priest of Hora. 5.
11. The statement of the thief Min-nekht son of Pentaur of the necropolis.
12. The merchant Pa-nekht-em-nut, of the Fayum. 5.
13. The merchant Nes-su-sebeka of Mer-sen-ari of the Fayum, gold 1 *kiti*, copper 20.
14. The metal-worker Amen-heru-ab, of the necropolis, copper 3.
15. The sandal-maker Pa-abu-nekht, of the temple of Ra-user-maa-mery Amen (Ramses III) L.P.H., under the authority of the high priest of Amen. 3.
16. The sandal-maker Ashertu-khetu, of the temple of Ra-user-maa-mery Amen (Ramses III) L.P.H. 2.
17. The workman User-hat-meru, of the necropolis 2.
18. The woman Ta-ri-sepi, of the necropolis, the seamstress of the workman Hor-a. 1.
19. The woman Ta-ka-ary, of the necropolis. 1.

TRANSCRIPTION.

Page 3 (Plate X).

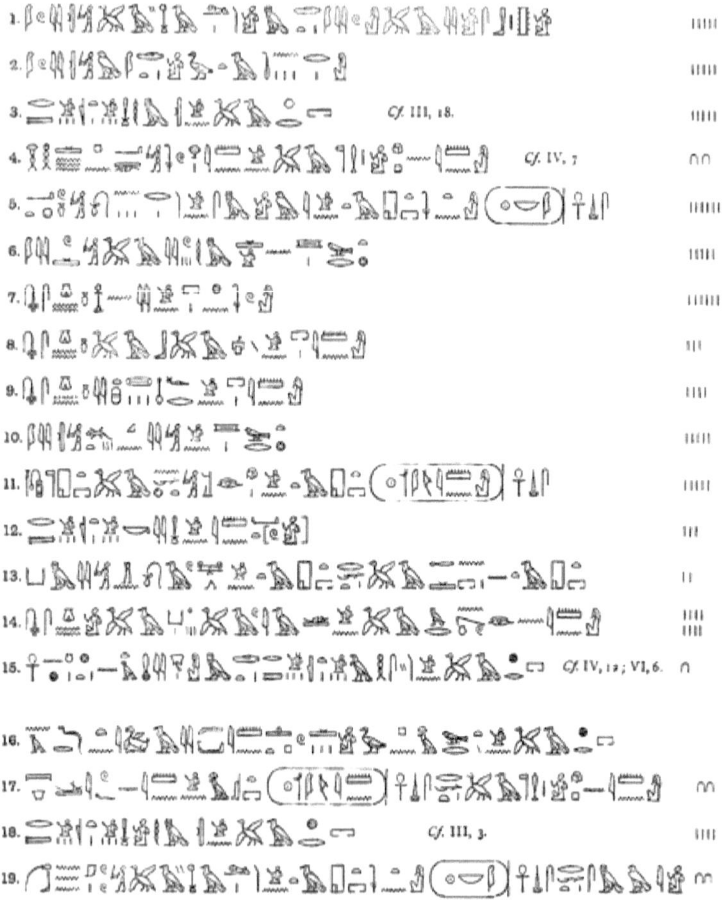

Transliteration.

III.

1. *shuy Pai-kha-ru em det shyu Pay-seb* 5.
2. *shuy Ḥer-maā-det mes ne Ta-thenu-ry* 5.
3. *reth ḳedet Sen-nezem ne pa kher* 5.
4. *uaḥ Penā-nekht-su-ḥer-Ȧmen ne pa neter ḥen tepi ne Ȧmen* 20.
5. *atekhu Ua-nu-re ne sem Ḥerā ne ta ḥat seten (Ra-neb-maā)‖ A.U.S.* 6.
6. *shyu Payu-nezem ne Mer-ur* 5.
7. *pefes-genen Sheny ne per Khensu* 5.
8. *pefes-genen Pa-be-pasa ne per Ȧmen* 3.
9. *pefes-genen Y-tau-nefer ne per Ȧmen* 5.
10. *shy Ȧshertu-ḳeny ne Mer-ur* 5.
11. *sesh neter ḥat Pa-nekht-resu-tep ne ta ḥat (Rā-user-maā mery Ȧmen)‖ Ȧ.U.S.* 5.
12. *reth ḳedet Ky-sen ne Ȧmen-nekhtu* 3.
13. *kamy Ȧn-uau ne ta ḥat er khet pa ad ne per ne ta ḥat* 2.
14. *pefes-genen Pa-kau-pauāa ne pa mer nenu ne Ȧmen* 8.
15. *ānkh ne nut ne Ta-muy em det reth ḳedet Neḥesī ne pa kher* 10.
16. *na zedet ne āzay Ȧmen-ḥetepu sa Pen-ta-ur ne pa kher*
17. *ḥer usekh Auf-ne-Ȧmen ne ta āst (Rā-user-maā mery Ȧmen)‖ A.U.S. er khet pay neter ḥen tepi ne Ȧmen* 20.
18. *reth ḳedet Sen-nezem ne pa kher* 4.
19. *uāb ḥenntun Pai-kharu ne ta ḥat seten (Rā-neb maā)‖ A.U.S. er khet sem Ḥeni* 20.

Translation.

III.

1. The merchant Paï-kha-ru in the hand of the merchant Pay-seba 5.
2. The merchant Hor-maa-det son of Ta-thenu-ri 5.
3. The workman Sen-nezem of the necropolis 5.
4. The water-carrier Pena-nekth-su-ḥer-Amen of the high priest of Amen 20.
5. The baker Ua-nu-ri of the sem-priest Hora of the temple of the king Ra-neb-maa (Amenhetep III) L.P.H. 6.
6. The merchant Payu-nezem of the Fayum 5.
7. The oil-boiler Sheny of the temple of Khonsu 6.
8. The oil-boiler Pa-be-pasa of the temple of Amen 3.
9. The oil-boiler Y-tau-nefer of the temple of Amen 5.
10. The merchant Ashertu-keny of the Fayum 5.
11. The scribe of the temple Pa-nekht-resu-tep of the temple of Ra-user-maa mery Amen (Ramses III) L.P.H. 5.
12. The workman Ky-sen of Amen-nekhtu 3.
13. The gardener Au-uau of the temple and under the authority of the major domo of the temple 2.
14. The oil-boiler Pa-kau-pauāa of the Superintendent of the huntsmen of Amen 8.
15. The woman Ta-muy in the hand of the workman Nehesi of the necropolis 10.
16. The statement of the thief Amenhetepu son of Pentaur of the necropolis
17. The boat-*reise* Auf-en-Amen of the temple of Ra-user-maa-mery-Amen L.P.H., under the authority of the high priest of Amen 20.
18. The workman Sen-nezem of the necropolis 4.
19. The *uab*-priest and metal worker Paï-kha-ru of the temple of the king Ra-neb-maa (Amen heten III) L.P.H., under the authority of the *sem*-priest Hora 20.

TRANSCRIPTION.

Page 4 (Plate XI).

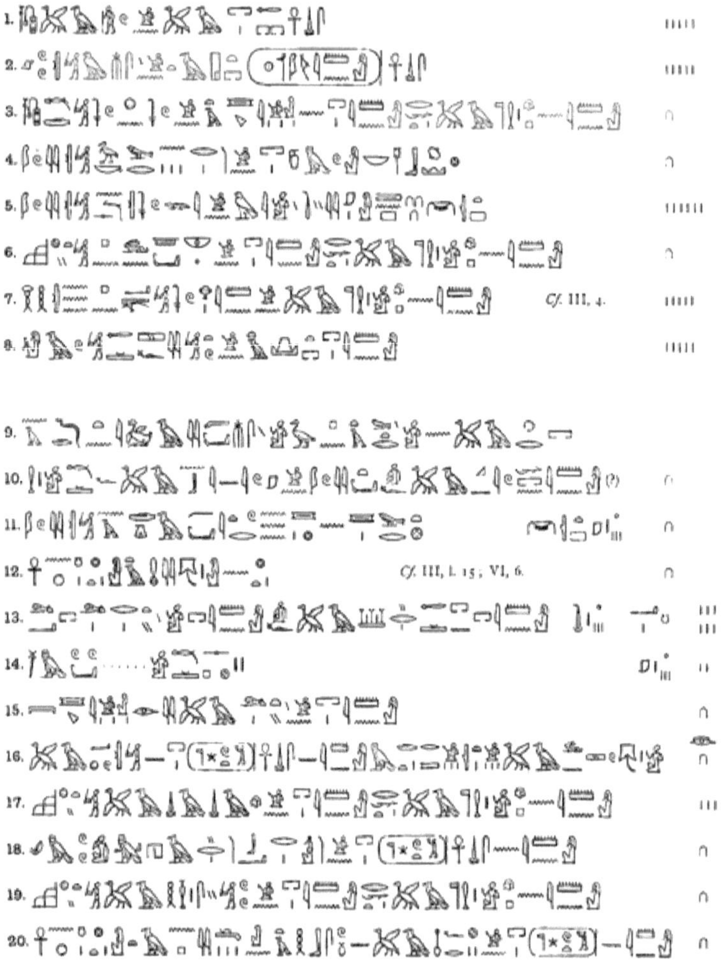

Transliteration.

IV.

1. *sesh Pa-seru ne pa per perui-aā A.U.S.* 5.
2. *khentuu Her-mes ne ta ḥat (Rā-user-maā mery Āmen)| A.U.S.* 5.
3. *sesh Shed-su-khensu ne ta merā ne per Āmen er khet pa neter ḥen tepī ne Āmen* 10.
4. *shuy Bak-ur-nu-re ne per Khnemu neb ābu* 10.
5. *shuy Nes-su-sebekā ne Ḥerā mes [ne] Thiy ḥemt deben 30 nub ḳedet* 6.
6. *sekheti Pen-un-ḥeb ne per Āmen er khet pa neter ḥen tepī ne Āmen* 10.
7. *waḥ Penā-nekth-su-ḥer-Āmen ne pa neter ḥen tepī ne Āmen* 5.
8. *sau Aā-shefy-nekhtu ne ta shent [ne] per Āmen* 5.
9. *ma zedet ne āzay Mes sa Pen-ta-ur ne pa kher*
10. *ḥen Meḥ-ef-pa-neb ānā ne shuyt ḥems ef pa ḳenāu ne Āmen* 10.
11. *shuy Na-dega [ne] ātera ne Mer-ur neb ḳedet ḥemt* 10.
12. *ānkh ne nut ne Ta-māy ne nut* 10.
13. *ār Ru-re-tī [ne] per Āmen nekhen-ef pa-shaī-re aā per ne per Āmen ḥesment . . . . .* 6.
14. *uḥemuu . . . . neḥ sep ḥemt* 2.
15. *ḥer merā Āry-pa-ru-tī ne per Āmen* 10.
16. *pa ākhua ne per (neter-duat) A.U.S. ne Āmen em det reth ḳedet Pa-unshu* 10.
17. *sekheti Pa-zaza ne per Āmen er khet pa neter ḥen tepī ne Āmen* 4.
18. *sedemuu Mā-ḥairu-bāru ne per (neter-duat) A.U.S. ne Āmen* 10.
19. *sekhetī Pa-ḥesīu ne per Āmen er khet pa neter ḥen tepī ne Āmen* 10.
20. *ānkh ne nut Ta-nepy ne ta ḥebsu ne Pa-nefer-sepi ne per (neter-duat)| ne Āmen* 10.

Translation.

IV.

1. The scribe Pa-seru of the house of Pharaoh L.P.H. 5.
2. The baker Her-mes of the temple of Ra-user-maa-mery-Amen (Ramses III) L.P.H. 5.
3. The scribe Shed-su-khonsu of the canal workers of the house of Amen and under the authority of the high priest of Amen 10.
4. The merchant Bak-ur-nu-ri of the temple of Khnem Lord of Elephantine 10.
5. The merchant Nes-su-sebekā of Hora born of Thiy. Copper 30 deben, gold 1 kiti.
6. The weaver Pen-un-heb of the house of Amen under the authority of the high priest of Amen 10.
7. The water carrier Pena-nekht-su-her-amen of the high priest of Amen 5.
8. The guardian Aa-shefy-nekhtu of the granaries of the house of Amen 5.
9. The statement of the thief Mes son of Pentaur of the necropolis.
10. The slave Meh-ef-pa-neb an-au of the merchant sitting in the kenau of the house of Amen 10.
11. The merchant Na-dega of Ateru in the Fayum. Gold 1 *kiti* copper 10.
12. The woman Ta-māy of the city 10.
13. The storehouse [keeper] Ru-ri-ti of the house of Amen, and (?) . Pa-shairi major domo of the house of Amen. Copper 6.
14. The reporter . . (?) . . . Copper 10.
15. The chief of the canal workers Ary-pa-ru-ti of the house of Amen 10.
16. The baker of the house of divine worship L.P.H., of Amen in the hand of the workman Pa-unshu 10.
17. The weaver Pazaza of the house of Amen under the authority of the high priest of Amen 4.
18. The hearer (? judge) Ma-hairu-baru of the house of divine worship L.P.H., of Amen 10.
19. The weaver Pahesiu of the house of Amen under the authority of the high priest of Amen 10.
20. The woman Ta-nepy of the seamstress of Pa-nefer-sepi of the house of divine worship of Amen 10.

TRANSCRIPTION.

Page 5 (Plate XII).

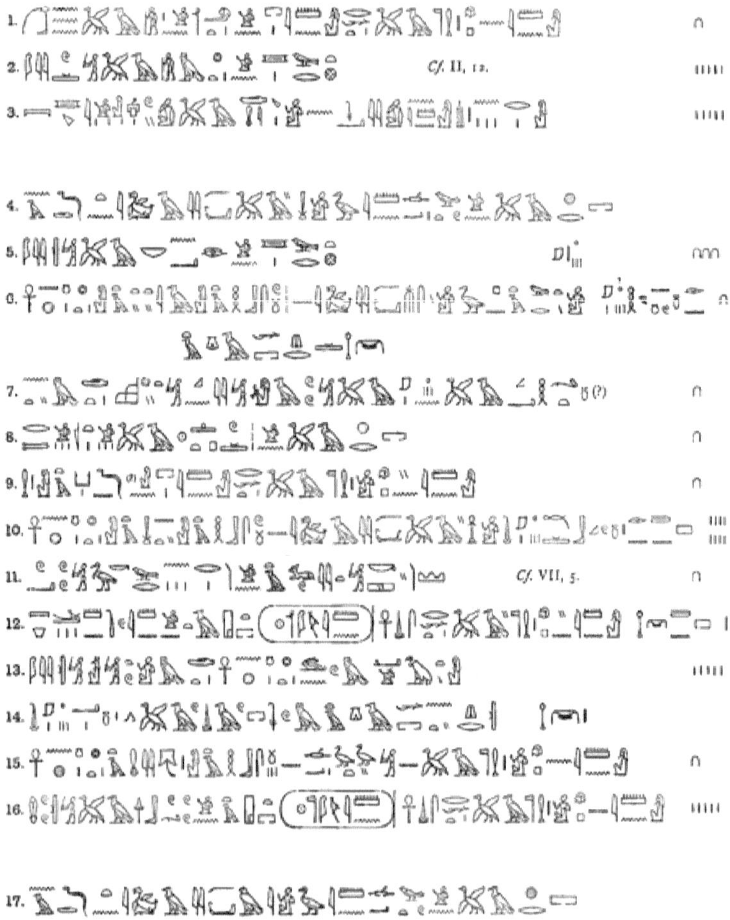

Transliteration.

V.

1. *uab Pa-ser ne User-ḥāt ne per Ȧmen er khet pa neter ḥen tepi ne Ȧmen* 10.
2. *shyu Pa-ser-em-nut ne Mer-ur* 5.
3. *ḥer merá Sauī-pa-demá ne ḥen-iy ne Ȧmen Ȧn-nu-re* 5.
4. *na zedet ne ȧzay Paī-sen sa Ȧmen-uā-shertu ne pa kher.*
5. *shyu Pa-neb-nā ne Mer-ur . ḥemt* 30.
6. *ȧnkh ne nut Ta-ti-ti-ȧa ta ḥeben ne ȧzay Mes sa Pen-ta-ur ḥemt ḥenu ur ne 10 ta ga kherī ḥez nub.*
7. *neti em det sekhetī Ḳeny suun Pa ḥemt ne pa ḳuḥt* 10.
8. *rekh ḳedet pa-ru-ḥetepu ne pa kher* 10.
9. *ḥen Ta-ka-zen ne per Ȧmen er khet pa neter ḥen tepī ne Ȧmen* 10.
10. *ȧnkh ne nut Ta-senti ta ḥeben ne ȧzay Paī-shenz ḥesmen meḥ beḳu ȧr deben* 8.
11. *mȧua Bak-ur-nu-re ne ta auyt keshi* 10.
12. *ḥer uesekh Menthu-ȧmen ne ta ḥat (Rā-user-maā mery-Ȧmen)| A.U.S. er khet paī neter ḥen tepī ne Ȧmen . ḥez nub deben* 1.
13. *shy Set-nekhtu em det ȧnkh ne nut Unu-em-de-ȧ-mut* 5.
14. *ḥesmen ā ȧu pa uzau su em ta gat netī kher ḥez nub* 1.
15. *ȧnkh ne nut Ta-māy ta ḥeben ne uā rekhtī ne pa neter ḥen tepī ne Ȧmen* 10.
16. *debu Pa-abu ne ta ḥat (Rā-user-maā mery-ȧmen)| A.U.S. er khet pa neter ḥen tepī ne Ȧmen* 5.
17. *na zedet ne azay Ḥeru sa Ȧmen-uā-shert ne pa kher.*

Translation.

V.

1. The *uab*-priest Pa-ser of User-hat of the house of Amen and under the authority of the high priest of Amen 10.
2. The merchant Pa-ser-em-nut of the Fayum 5.
3. The chief of the canal workers Sauï-pa-demá of the musician of Amen An-nu-ri 5.
4. The statement of the thief Paï-sen son of Amen-uā-shertu of the necropolis.
5. The merchant Pa-neb-nā of the Fayum. Copper 30.
6. The woman Ta-ti-ti-áa the clothes of the thief Mes son of Pentaur. Copper vases making 10 . . . . silver.
7. He who is in the hand of the weaver Keny and the guardian Pa. Copper of the *kuh*-vase. 1. 10.
8. The workman Pa-ru-hetepu of the necropolis. 10.
9. The slave Ta-ka-zen of the house of Amen under the authority of the high priest of Amen 10.
10. The woman Ta-senti the seamstress of the thief Paï-shenz. Bronze. A *baku*-vase making 8 deben.
11. The lieutenant Bak-ur-nu-ri of the soldiers of Ethiopia 10.
12. The boat-*reise* Mentu-amen of the temple of Ra-user-maa-mery-Amen (Ramses III) L.P.H., under the authority of the high priest of Amen. Silver 1 deben.
13. The merchant Set-nekht in the hand of the woman Un-em-det-á-mut 5.
14. Bronze out of the storehouse and of the *kat*-house which is in . . . . . . Silver. 1.
15. The woman Ta-māy, the seamstress of a washerman of the high priest of Amen 10.
16. The sandal-maker Pa-abu of the temple of Ra-user-maa-mery Amen (Ramses III) L.P.H., under the authority of the high priest of Amen 5.
17. The word of the thief Horu son of Amen-uā-shert of the necropolis.

TRANSCRIPTION.

Page 6 (Plate XIII).

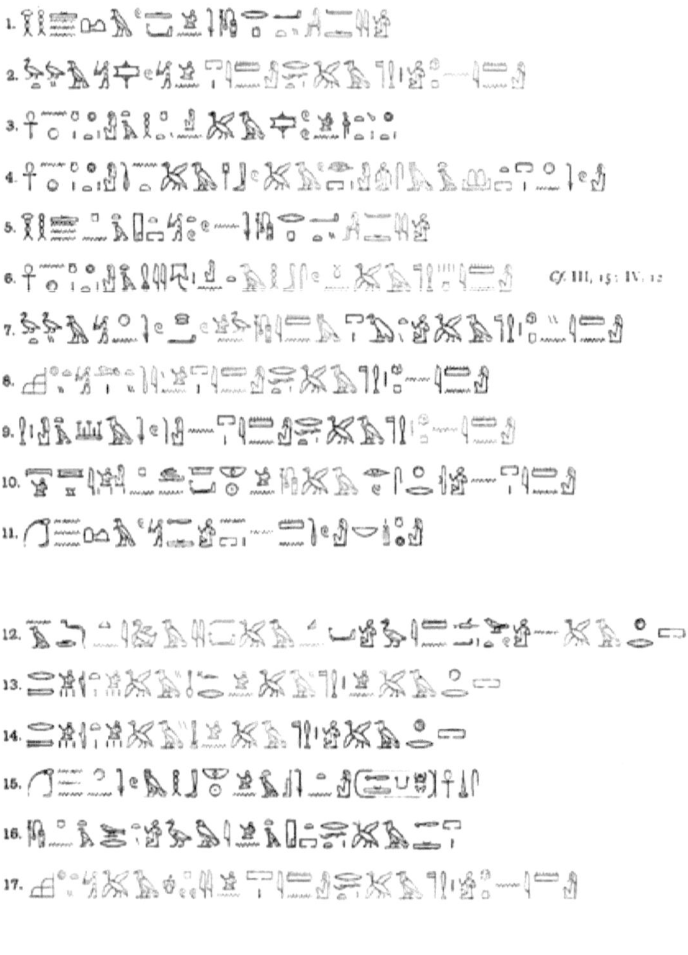

Cf. III, 15; IV, 12

Transliteration.

VI.

1. *uaḥ Aḥatiu ne seten sesh erpāti Ḥuy*
2. *rekhti Nefu ne per Åmen er khet pa neter ḥen tep ne Åmen*
3. *ānkh ne nut Ta-ḥenut-pa-nefu ne āmentet*
4. *ānkh ne nut Thent-pa-ābu-pau ḥems-es em ta shentui [ne] per khensu*
5. *uaḥ Pen-ta-ḥat-nekhtu ne seten sesh erpāti Ḥuy*
6. *ānkh ne nut Ta-māy ne ta ḥebau pa neter ḥen IV ne Åmen*
7. *rekhti Khensu-khāu sa ne sesh Åmen-em-per-mut, pa neter ḥen tepi ne Åmen*
8. *sekheti Ru-ti-tha ne per Åmen er khet pa neter ḥen tep ne Åmen*
9. *ḥen Ta-shasu ne per Åmen er khet pa neter ḥen tep ne Åmen*
10. *ḥer meri Pen-un-ḥeb ne sesh Pa-āru-sekher ne per Åmen*
11. *uab Aḥatiu-nā ne per ne Mentu neb Ånt*
12. *na zedet ne āzay Pa-ḥen sa Åmen-nā-sherlu ne pa kher*
13. *reth ḳedet Paī-nefer ne paī neter ḥen ne pa kher*
14. *reth ḳedet Paī-sen ne pa neter ḥen pa kher*
15. *uab Khensu-em heb ne ta āat seten per (uā-ka-kheper)| A.U.S.*
16. *sesh Pen-ta-ur sa Ḥerā ne ta ḥut er khet pa aā per*
17. *sekheti Pa-sa-pauy (?) ne per Åmen er khet pa neter ḥen tep ne Åmen*

Translation.

VI.

1. The water carrier Ahatiu of the royal scribe, the hereditary prince Huy
2. The washerman Nefu of the house of Amen under the authority of the high priest of Amen.
3. The woman Ta-henut-pa-nefu of the western city
4. The woman Thent-pa-abu-pau residing in the granaries of the temple of Khensu
5. The water-carrier Pen-ta-hatnu of the royal scribe; the hereditary prince Huy
6. The woman Ta-maä of the seamstress of the fourth priest of Amen
7. The washerman Khensu-khau son of the scribe Amen-em-per-mut of the high priest of Amen
8. The weaver Ru-ti-tha of the house of Amen and under the authority of the high priest of Amen
9. The female slave Ta-shasu of the house of Amen and under the authority of the high priest of Amen
10. The chief of the canal workers, Pen-un-heb of the scribe Pa-aru-sekher of the house of Amen
11. The *uab*-priest Ahatiu-na of the temple of Mentu lord of Erment.
12. The statement of the thief Pa-ken son of Amen-nā-sherta of the necropolis
13. The workman Pai-nefer of the high priest of the necropolis
14. The workman Pai-sen of the priest of the necropolis
15. The uab-priest Khensu-em-heb of the domain(?) of the king [Ra]-aa-kheper-Ka (Thothmes II) L.P.H.
16. The scribe Pen-ta-ur son of Hora of the temple and under the authority of the major domo
17. The weaver Pa-sa-pauy of the house of Amen and under the authority of the high priest of Amen

TRANSCRIPTION.

Page 7 (Plate XIV).

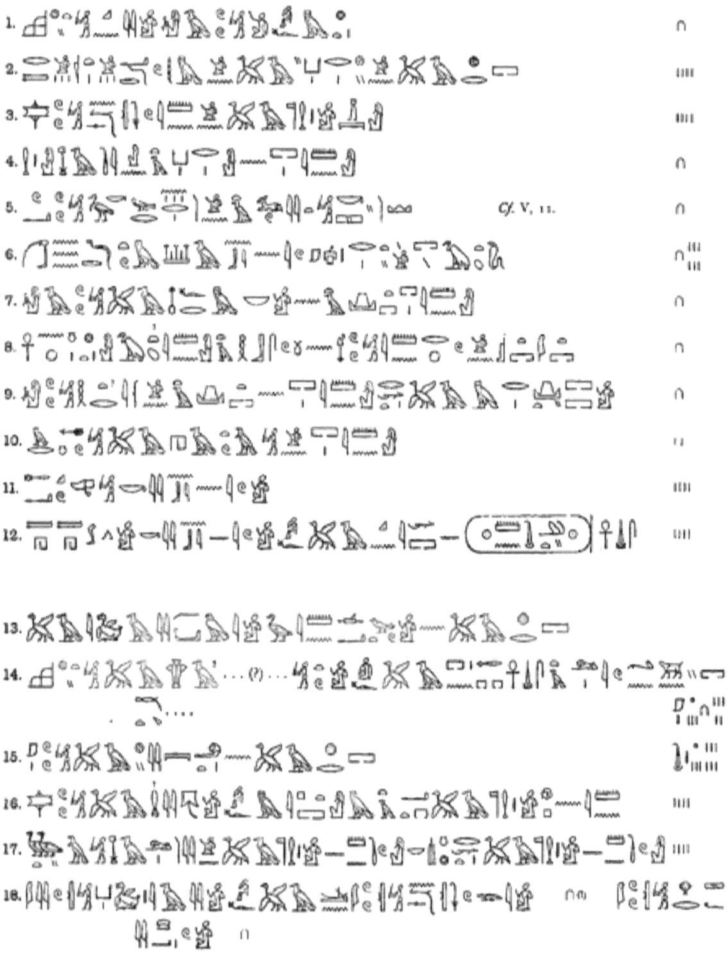

Page 8 (Plate XIV).

Transliteration.

VII.

1. *sekheti Ḳeny sauu ḥems-ef em nut* 10.
2. *reth ḥedet Azedu-nezem ne Pai-ka-ri-sepi ne pa kher* 4.
3. *nefun Nes-su-Ȧmen ne pa neter ḥen [ne] Ȧnḥer* 4.
4. *ḥen Kha-thi ne Ta-ka-ri ne per Amen*
5. *idnu Bak-ur-nu-ri ne ta anyt keshi* 10.
6. *uab Zed-tu-em-sha-nebin ȧu-sa-ri-ti [ne] per Mut* 16.
7. *sauu Pa-nefer-em-neb ne ta shenta [ne] per Ȧmen* 10.
8. *ānkh ne nut Mat (?) Ȧmen ta ḥeben ne ḥemti Ȧmen-rekhu ne ȧst Maāt* 10.
9. *sauu Ḥeteru (?) ne ta shent ne per Ȧmen er khet pa mer shentiui* 10.
10. *mer sunu Pa-ḥa tu-ti (?) ne per Ȧmen* 10.
11. *khāku Ky-ne bȧn ȧu* 4.
12. *theh-theh Ky-ne bȧn au ne ḥems-ef pa ḥemi (Rā-men-pehti) A.U.S.* 4.
13. *pa ȧzay Ḥerȧ sa Ȧmen-uā-shert ne pa-kher*
14. *sekhti Pa-ḥa? . . . . nekhtu? ḥems ef em per ne perai ȧt A.U.S. Ta-ru-ȧu ne kheni mekt . . . . ḥemt* 15.
15. *ḥemtuu Pa-sepiy-ḥer-ḥāt ne pa kher ḥesmen* 6.
16. *nefun Pa-may (?) ḥems-ef em ȧpt em ta ȧt [ne] . . . . pa neter ḥen tepi ne Amen* 4.
17. *rekhti Kha-ruy ne pa neter ḥen ne Mentu neb Ȧnu er khet pa neter ḥen ne Mentu* 4.
18. *shyu Ka-za-ȧay ḥems ef pa-usekh ne shuu Nes-su-sebekȧ* 10.
shuu Ḥer-shefy-khāu 10.

VIII.

1. *shuyuu An-nu-ri-ȧay ne Mer-ur* 5.
2. *ānkh ne nut Ȧn-nu-ry ne Ȧmentet* 5.

Translation.

VII.

1. The weaver Kony and the guardian residing in the city. 10.
2. The workman Azedu-nezem of Pai-ka-ri-sepi of the necropolis 4.
3. The boatman Nesi-su-Amen of the priest of Anher 4.
4. The female slave Kha-tha of Ta-ka-ri of the house of Amen 10.
5. The lieutenant Bak-ur-nu-ri of the Ethiopian soldiers 10.
6. The *ueb*-priest Zed-tu-em-sha-neban au-sa-ri-ti of the temple of Mut 16.
7. The guardian Pa-nefer-em-neb of the granary of the temple of Amen 10.
8. The woman Amen, the seamstress of the craftsman Amen-rekhu of the Place of Maat 10.
9. The guardian Hetera (?) of the granary of the temple of Amen under the authority of the overseer of the granaries 10.
10. The Superintendent of the doctors Pa-hatu-ti (?) of the house of Amen 10.
11. The barber Ky-ne ban au 4.
12. (?) . . . . Ky-ne ban au residing in (?) the *kena* of Ra-men-pehti (Ramses I) L.P.H. 4.
13. the thief Hora son of Amen-ua-shert of the necropolis
14. The weaver Pa-ha . . . . nekhtu . . . . . . residing in (?) the house of Pharaoh L.P.H., the . . . . . of the interior of the north, copper 15.
15. The metal worker Pa-sepiy-her-hat of the necropolis bronze 6.
16. The boatman Pa-may residing in the division of the department of the high priest of Amen 4.
17. The washerman Kha-ruy of the priest of Mentu lord of Erment and under the authority of the priest of Mentu 4.
18. The merchant Ka-za-aay residing in the boat (?) of the merchant Nes-su-sebeka 10.
The merchant Her-shefy-khau 10.

VIII.

1. The merchant An-nu-re-aay of the Fayum 5.
2. The woman An-nu-re of the western city 5.

C. GEOGRAPHICAL PAPYRUS.

PAPYRUS No. VIII.

(PLATES XV–XVIII.)

FRAGMENTS of a papyrus about 5 feet in length by $10\frac{1}{4}$ inches high relating to the geography of Egypt and the Fayûm. It is written in small and clear hieroglyphic handwriting, and perhaps originally formed part of a second roll of the Great Fayûm Geographical treatise, portions of which are preserved in the Gizeh Museum and among the private collection of Mr. Hood, of Nettleham Hall, in Lincolnshire.

It is impossible, however, to fit the Amherst fragments on to the pieces now known, but the papyrus itself relates to the same subject and is written in the same handwriting as the Gizeh and Hood documents.

On a small strip at Nettleham Hall, recently published by Lanzoni, occurs the cartouche of one of the Ptolemies (? Euergetes II), thus dating the document to Ptolemaic times.

The first half of the papyrus (Pls. XV–XVI) is divided into eight vertical columns, each being subdivided horizontally into five compartments containing figures of the crocodile-god Sebek. To the right of each figure is written the name of the god and of the nome or locality over which he was supposed to preside. In several cases the place-names have been destroyed: in the following list of the nomes of Upper Egypt I have, for completeness sake, inserted between brackets these destroyed names.

PLATE XV.—THE NOMES OF LOWER EGYPT.

COLUMN I.

[No. 1. *Ta-Khent*, Nubia.]

,, 2. *Thes-Heru*, the Apollinopolite Nome.

,, 3. *Ten*, the Latopolite Nome.

,, 4. *Mert-rá*, the Theban Nome.

,, 5. *Herui*, the Coptite Nome.

COLUMN II.

[,, 6. *A-du*, the Tentyrite Nome.]

,, 7. *Sekhem*, the Diospolite Nome.

,, 8. *Abez*, the Thinite Nome.

[,, 9. *Min*, the Panopolite Nome.]

,, 10. *Uazt*, the Aphroditopolite Nome.

Column III.

No. 11. [*Set*], the Hypselite Nome. It is interesting to note that the name of Set is not inserted in the papyrus, doubtless owing to the religious scruples of the ancient scribe.

„ 12. *Du-ef*, the Antaeopolite Nome.

„ 13. *Atef-Khent*, the Lykopolite Nome.

„ 14. *Atef peh*, the Northern Lykopolite Nome, of which Cusae was the capital.

„ 15. *Unt*, the Hermopolite Nome.

Column IV.

[„ 16. *Mahez*, the Northern Hermopolite Nome, the Oryx Nome of earlier times.]

[„ 17. *Anup*, the Cynopolite Nome.]

[„ 18. *Srp*, the Eastern Oxyrrhynchite Nome.]

„ 19. *Het-seten*, the metropolis (?) of *Uaseb*, the Western Oxyrrhynchite Nome.

„ 20. *Henen-Seten*, Heracleopolis, the capital of *Am-Khent*, the Heracleopolite Nome.

PLATE XVI.—THE FAYÛM AND NOMES OF LOWER EGYPT.

Column I.

The first place-name is destroyed: it should probably be restored *Ta-she*, the Nomos Arsinoites, or El Fayûm. In the second compartment occurs the name of *Shedet*, Crocodilopolis, the capital of the Fayûm. With the third compartment begins the list of the Nomes of Lower Egypt which are not all arranged geographically, nor in accordance with other Nome lists of Ptolemaic times. The following numbers therefore refer to the compartments of the respective columns, and not to the number of the Nomes.

No. 3. *Anbu-hez*, the Memphite or first Nome of Lower Egypt.

„ 4. *Sekhemt*, Letopolis, the chief town of the Letopolite or second Nome.

„ 5. *Ament*, the Libyan or third Nome.

Column II.

„ 1. *Sapi*, comprising the two Saïte Nomes, the fourth and fifth of Lower Egypt.

„ 2. *Ri-nefer*, the ονουφις of the Greek Geographers (*cf.* Brugsch, *Dict. Geog.*, p. 1017).

„ 3. *Bah*, the metropolis of the fifteenth Nome, *i.e.*, the Hermopolite Nome of the Delta.

„ 4. *Ham-hit*, the Mendesius Nome, the sixteenth Nome of Lower Egypt.

„ 5. *Theb-neter*, Sebennytos, the metropolis of the twelfth or Sebennytes Nome.

Column III.

„ 1 and 2. The place-names are destroyed.

„ 3. *Besth*, perhaps the metropolis of the seventh or Metelite Nome.

No. 4. *Zar*, Tanis, the capital of the fourteenth or Tanite Nome.

,, 5. *Heq-àt*, the thirteenth or Heliopolite Nome.

Column IV.

,, 1. *Sam-ḥud*, the seventeenth or Diospolite Nome.

,, 2. [ ] *Het-*[*Uart* ?, Avaris ?].

,, 3. *Per Bast*, Bubastes, the capital of the eighteenth of Bubastite Nome.

,, 4. *Ámt*, Buto, the capital of the nineteenth or Buticus Nome.

,, 5. *Ta-remt*, *i.e.*, "the land of fish," probably the lake region around Menzaleh.

PLATE XVII.

The left-hand fragment on Pl. XVII joins on to the right-hand fragment on Pl. XVI, and refers to SEBEK SHEDET, the god of the Fayûm.

The right-hand fragment of Pl. XVII contains three complete and the halves of two other vertical columns of hieroglyphics. The inscription names the goddess Isis in connection with the myth of Sebek, and that god's connection with *Ta-she*, the Fayûm.

PLATE XVIII.

To the left is a mutilated picture of the *ḥat neter net sh̲ent Neith*, "Temple of the acacia of the goddess Neith." An archer drawing a bow with arrow is represented in the shrine, behind which is depicted an acacia tree; the whole scene is surrounded by a canal or moat.

In the centre of the page is a mythical description of the region called Shent-Neith, beginning: *ast ten sh̲end Neith pu ren ef áu ges neter ḥat ne Sebek neb Ri-seh*, "This locality bears the name Shend-Neith (*i.e.*, the acacia of the goddess Neith). It is at the side of the temple of Sebek, Lord of Ri-seh."

To the right is represented a canal in the form of and eight mythical personages, those to the left being KEK and his consort KEKET and HEH and HEHET, whilst those to the right are NUT and NUT (the female) and [ ]? AMEN and AMENT

D. MYTHICAL PAPYRUS.

PAPYRUS No. IX. (The Astarte Papyrus.)

(PLATES XIX–XXI.)

Fragments of two pages and the lower part of three others, of a papyrus mentioning the goddess Astarte, written in a very clear and neat bieratic hand of the XIXth or XXth dynasty. How and when it came into the possession of Lord Amherst is not known, but it was already in his collection in 1871, when Dr. Samuel Birch published a short account of it in the *Zeitschrift für Aegyptische Sprache* (pp. 119, 120). The subject appears to be certain "tribute of the sea" which was paid to the Phœnician goddess Astarte by (?) a messenger of Ptah, but the papyrus is unfortunately too fragmentary to permit of any connected translation being made.

E. ACCOUNTS AND MISCELLANEOUS PAPYRI.

PAPYRUS No. X.

Fragments of a papyrus written in the hieratic writing of the Middle Kingdom, apparently containing some accounts relating to flax, domestic animals, etc. It is probable that these fragments once belonged to the great account papyrus of Gizeh (*Boulac Papyri*, No. 18), but unfortunately they cannot now be fitted into their original places. On the smallest fragment occurs the name of SEBEK-HETEP. On the second we read :—

Ar-[de-]ek nef, "If thou givest him

meh, flax

ar-[de-]ek nef, If thou givest him

meh, flax

shed em uza, taken out of the magazine

medetu aut, stall oxen

shasha heq 15, 15 heq of beads

àm ren ef ne zazat, name list of the auditors

sesh ne zazat, the scribe of the auditors"

Fragment I, height 5 inches, length 2¾ inches.
Fragment II, height 2 inches, length ¾ inch.

PAPYRUS No. XI.

(PLATE XXI. Nos. IV and V.)

Two fragments of an hieratic papyrus mentioning a building of Horemheb (the last king of the XVIIIth dynasty) in the temple of Amen. A similar building of Seti-mer-en-Ptah (Seti I), the second ruler of the XIXth dynasty, is mentioned in the first fragment in the right hand top corner. These two fragments evidently belong to the series of accounts of the time of Seti I, preserved in the Museum of the Louvre and published by Spiegelberg in his *Rechnungen aus der Zeit Seti I*, but they do not fit exactly with any of the fragments in Paris.

PLATE XXI. No. IV.

1. [*peryt*] *perui aa A.U.S.*
2. *er ges per (Heru-em-heb) em per Amen*
3. *ash heri aù en meh* XL
4. *ash heri ne meh* XXXV
5. *ash shemshemu her Khetemu*

1. Estates (?) of the Pharaoh L.P.H.
2. [near (?)] the house of Hor-em-heb in the temple of Amen

3. Great beam of cypress of 40 cubits . . .
4. Beam of cypress of 35 cubits
5. *Shemshemu* of cypress on the seal ?

PLATE XXI. No. V.

1.  ". . . of the house of Seti-mery [ne] Ptah.

2.  . . . the house of Hor-em-heb in the temple of Amen."

PAPYRUS No. XII.

Fragment of a papyrus in a very curious hieratic character of about the XIXth dynasty, of uncertain character and much mutilated.

Length $5\frac{1}{2}$ inches by $4\frac{3}{4}$ inches high.

PAPYRUS No. XIII.

Fragment of an hieratic papyrus apparently of about the same date as No. XII. Of uncertain character. Much mutilated.

Length 6 inches by $4\frac{1}{2}$ inches high.

PAPYRUS No. XIV.

Fragment of a papyrus written in the hieratic character, apparently of about the XIXth dynasty. The contents were perhaps of a literary character, but it is too mutilated to read or transcribe.

Length $11\frac{1}{2}$ inches by $3\frac{1}{4}$ inches wide.

PAPYRUS No. XV.

Fragment of a very mutilated papyrus, written in the hieratic character of the XIXth dynasty, containing fragments of a literary text of uncertain origin. Too much mutilated to decipher or transcribe.

Length $12\frac{1}{4}$ inches by 6 inches high.

F. RELIGIOUS PAPYRI: BOOKS OF THE DEAD.

(a.) HIEROGLYPHIC.

PAPYRUS No. XVI.

Papyrus of the *Sauti per-hez*, "guard of the treasury," *Nefer-renpet*, "Nefer-renpit." It contains parts of Chapters 1, 42, 54, 57, 58, 61, 63, 67, 75, 99, 105, 125, 127, 137, 144 *a–g*, 145 *a*, *f*, *m*, *n*, 149, *h*, *i*, *o*, and 152. It is written in large hieroglyphic writing and is illustrated by numerous well executed, but for the most part mutilated vignettes.

Period. XIXth Dynasty. [Seven sheets.]

PAPYRUS No. XVII.

(PLATE XXII.)

Papyrus of the *her sauti seshu ne neb tawi*, "Chief of the guardians (= Chief Librarian) of the writings of the lord of the two lands (*i.e.*, the king)," named *Khay*, "Khay." It contains parts of Chapters 1, 17, 91–93, 105, 110 *a*, 121, 124, 125, 136, 137, 144 and 145. The writing is large and bold and the papyrus contains some coloured vignettes. Another part of this papyrus is preserved in the British Museum (No. 9935 Lebri).

Period. XIXth Dynasty. Three sheets: the width of the papyrus being about 14½ inches.

PAPYRUS No. XVIII.

Papyrus of the *mer shentui ne neb tawi*, "Superintendent of the granaries of the Lord of the two lands" *Ptah-mes* "Ptahmes." It contains parts of Chapters 48, 51, 76, 82, 87 and 141, and upon the *verso* of the first fragment a line of large hieroglyphs (1½ inches in height) giving the name and titles of its original owner. It is unfortunately in a very mutilated condition.

Period. Late XVIIIth or early XIXth Dynasty. Two sheets. Width 2 feet 3 inches.

PAPYRUS No. XIX.

Papyrus of the *qemá ne Amen*, "Musician of Amen," *Nuby*, "Nuby," containing part of Chapter 146 of the *Book of the Dead*, written in the large hieroglyphic writing of the XIXth Dynasty. The name has been inserted by a different hand to the rest of the document. 1 page. Width 16 inches.

PAPYRUS No. XX.

Papyrus of *Rā-nefer*, "Ra-nefer," containing parts of Chapter 149 (*b*, *d*, *g*, *l*, *m*, *n*, *o*) of the *Book of the Dead*. The writing is hieroglyphic, but the script is smaller than that in the four preceding documents. The name Ra-nefer has been roughly inserted in a different handwriting to the rest of the manuscript.

Period. XIXth or early XXth Dynasty. Width 13 inches.

PAPYRUS No. XXI.

Papyrus of the , *ḥen neter Ȧmen Rā seten neteru*, "Priest of Amen Ra, king of the gods" , *Nesi-ȧmen*, "Nesi-Amen," containing the vignette of Chapter 125 of the *Book of Dead*. XXIInd Dynasty. 1 page. Width 7 inches.

PAPYRUS No. XXII.

(PLATE XXIII.)

Papyrus of , *Pede-ḥeru*, "Pede-heru," born of the , *nebt per Du-nes-nes*, "Lady of the house, Durnesnes." It contains parts of Chapters 11–13, 37, 38, 41, 79, 91–94, 108, 109, 145 *f–h*, *k–l*, and the vignette of Chapter 165 of the *Book of the Dead*. The writing is hieroglyphic and very small, but beautifully executed, and the vignettes are of considerable merit. XXVIth Dynasty. Width 8¾ inches. 8 sheets.

PAPYRUS No. XXIII.

Papyrus of the , *ḥen neter ne Ȧmen Rā seten neteru*, "Priest of Amen-Ra, king of the gods" , *Ym-hetep*, "Im-hetep," son of , *Aah-mes*, "Aahmes," also a priest of Amen-Ra, by the *nebt per ȧḥy ne Ȧmen-Rā*, "Lady of the house and chantress of Amen-Ra, , *Ta-ḵhred-ȧḥ*, "Ta-khred-ah." It contains Chapters 15 (*a* and *b*) and 89, with rough vignettes. The writing is hieroglyphic, but small, and of an inferior hand. XXVIth Dynasty. Width 14 inches.

PAPYRUS No. XXIV.

Papyrus of , *Ḥeru-se-ȧst*, "Hor-se-Isis," containing fragments of Chapters 15 and 18 of the *Book of the Dead*, written in large and well-formed hieroglyphics. The original height and length of this document cannot be ascertained, as only some thirty fragments of the lower part of the scroll are preserved. XXVIth Dynasty or later.

PAPYRUS No. XXV.

Papyrus, with a blank space left for the name of the purchaser to be inserted, written in the large hieroglyphic writing of the XVIIIth or XIXth dynasty, and containing portions of Chapters 32, 33, 41, 42, 63, 77, 82, 85–89, 98, 99, 105, and 121 of the *Book of the Dead*. 2 sheets.

PAPYRUS No. XXVI.

Another Papyrus, with a blank space left for the name of the purchaser to be inserted, written in large hieroglyphic writing of the XVIIIth or XIXth dynasty, and containing parts of Chapters of the *Book of the Dead*. In very bad preservation, but the remains of the vignettes show that it must once have been a magnificent document. 3 sheets.

PAPYRUS No. XXVII.

Papyrus of *Ḥeru*, "Horus," written in very small hieroglyphic writing, and containing part of Chapter 77 of the *Book of the Dead*. The manuscript is much mutilated, and consists of a small roll 3 inches in height, and 16 fragments. XXVIth Dynasty (?).

PAPYRUS No. XXVIII.

Papyrus of *Ta-de-nefer-ḥetep*, "Ta-de-nefer-hetep," born of the *nebt-per*, "Lady of the house," *Ta-rekh-es*, "Ta-rekh-es." It contains Chapter 18 of the *Book of the Dead* with the usual vignette. The writing is hieroglyphic, and nearly the same style as that of No. XXII (see Pl. XXIII).

The vignette is in outline only, without colour. 1 page.

Saitic. Height, 10½ inches, by 7½ inches in width; 19 inches long.

PAPYRUS No. XXIX.

Papyrus of the *neter ḥen ne Ámen*, "Priest of Amen," *Nesi-Ámen*, "Nesi-amen." Only some very roughly executed vignettes and the name of the owner of this manuscript are preserved. 1 page. 36 inches long by 9 inches high, and numerous fragments. XXVI Dynasty.

PAPYRUS No. XXX.

Papyrus of *Ser*, "Ser," born of *Ást-urt*, "Isis-urt," containing the vignette of Chapter 110 of the *Book of the Dead*. 1 page. 15½ inches by 14½ inches high. XXVI Dynasty.

PAPYRUS No. XXXI.

Twenty-six fragments of linen, with Chapters 13 (?) and 145, written for an individual named Nefer-Tum, in small cursive hieroglyphic characters.

PAPYRUS No. XXXII.

Papyrus containing part of the vignette of Chapter 110. The name of the person for whom it was written is not preserved. There are two fragments: one measuring 8 inches wide by 7 inches high; the other 7 inches wide by 5 inches high.

PAPYRUS No. XXXIIIa.

Fragments of a papyrus containing certain chapters of the *Book of the Dead* written in hieroglyphs. 1 page and 23 fragments. XIXth Dynasty.

PAPYRUS No. XXXIIIb.

Twenty fragments of another similar papyrus without name. XXth Dynasty.

(*b*.) HIERATIC.

PAPYRUS No. XXXIV.

Papyrus of the *Áḥy ne Ámen-Rā*, "Sistrum player of Amen-Ra," and *ḥen neter Maāt*, "Priest of Maat," *Nes-pa-kher-taui-es*, "Nes-pa-kher-taui-es." His mother's name was *Ta-Khabes*, "Ta-Khabes," but the father's name is not preserved. Parts of Chapters 7, 9, 12, 15, 27, 28, 125, 145, 146, 148, 149 (*a*, *e*), 150, 151, 152, 154, 157, 159, 161–165, are preserved. The texture of this papyrus is exceptionally fine, and the writing, a small and neat hieratic, is very good. XXIInd Dynasty.

PAPYRUS No. XXXV.

(PLATE XXIV.)

Papyrus of the *ḥen neter ne Ámen-em-ápt*, "Priest of Amen-in-Karnak," *Heru-nesti-ātef-ef*, "Hor-nesti-atef-ef," son of the *ḥen neter ne Khensu*, "Priest of Khonsu," *Heru-shetekh-ḥeru-nest*, "Hor-shetekh-hor-nest," by the *nebt per āḥyt ne Āmen*, "Lady of the house and chantress of Amen," *Nefer-ḥetep*, "Nefer-hetep." Hor-nesti-atef-ef also held the following titles in addition to that of Priest of Amen-in-Karnak :—

ḥen neter Ḥeru, "Priest of Horus."

ḥen neter ne Khensu, "Priest of Khonsu."

ḥen neter ne Āst, "Priest of Isis."

ḥen neter ne Ānup, "Priest of Anubis."

ḥen ḥez, "Servant of the white crown."

This magnificent papyrus is written in the small hieratic character of the XXIInd dynasty, and is elaborately illustrated with vignettes, one of them being brilliantly coloured. It is not complete, only about fourteen pages being in the Amherst Collection. It originally measured about 16 feet in length; the height of the papyrus being 1 foot 6 inches. The first part, containing about 30 chapters, is preserved in the British Museum (No. 10,037 [Salt 829]).* These chapters are 1–9, 12, 15–21, 23, 24, 26, 33–38, 40, 42, 48, and 49. The Amherst pieces contain Chapters 110 *a*, 111, 113, 114 *a*, 115, 117–120, 121 (the beginning only), 122, 125 (the end only, ll. 58–69), 125 *d*, 126, 128, 129, 132, 135, 137, 138, 148 *b*, 152, 154, 155, 157–159, 159 *bis*, and 161.

Period: XXIInd dynasty. 8 feet long by 1 foot 6 inches high.

* In the *Catalogue of the Collection of Egyptian Antiquities, the property of the late Henry Salt, Esq.* (London, 1835), p. 64), this papyrus is described as "a magnificent and perfect document in hieratic character, ornamented with numerous figures most delicately executed in black .... It is 18 inches wide and about 16 feet in length. From Thebes."

PAPYRUS No. XXXVI.

Papyrus of *Tahuti-sedem*, "Tahuti-sedem," son of the Lady *Thāmen*, "Tha-Āmen." It is written in small hieratic characters, and contains parts of Chapters 1, 7, 11, 15, 16, and 18. 1 page and 10 fragments. Græco-Roman period.

PAPYRUS No. XXXVII.

Papyrus of *Se-rā-taui*, "Se-ra-taui," son of the Lady *Āst-urt*, "Ast-urt," a sistrum player of Amen-Ra. 27 fragments. XXIInd Dynasty.

PAPYRUS No. XXXVIII.

Papyrus of the *ḥen neter ne Āmen*, "Priest of Amen," *Nesi-su-Āmen-em-āpt*, "Nesi-su-Amen-em-apt." It is written in the hieratic writing of the XXIInd dynasty, and contains the greater part of Chapter No. 1, with a mutilated vignette depicting the deceased. 3 pages. 26 inches, by 10 inches high. [Lee *Catalogue*, 431.] Græco-Roman period.

PAPYRUS No. XXXIX.

Papyrus of an 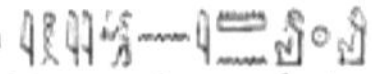 *āhy ne Àmen-Rā*, "sistrum player of Amen-Ra," whose name is unfortunately destroyed. It is written in the small hieratic of the XXVIth dynasty. [Lee, *Catalogue*, 435.]

PAPYRUS No. XL.

Papyrus containing some chapters of the *Book of the Dead* in a very careless and cursive hieratic, too illegible to read. Roman. [Lee, *Catalogue*, 430.]

PAPYRUS No. XLI.

Chapter 57 of the Book of the Dead, written in very cursive hieratic upon a piece of mummy cloth. [Lee, *Catalogue*, No. 437.]

PAPYRUS No. XLII.

Papyrus written in hieratic writing, apparently containing a part of a Chapter of the *Book of the Dead*. Height 10 inches, length 19½ inches. [Gliddon.]

G. DEMOTIC PAPYRI.

PAPYRUS No. XLIII.

Two fragments of a demotic papyrus written in the small character of the later Ptolemaic period. The fragments measure: No. 1, 8½ inches long by 8 inches high. No. 2, 4½ inches long by 5½ inches high.

PAPYRUS No. XLIV.

Eight small fragments of demotic writing.

PAPYRUS No. XLV.

Fragments of a demotic papyrus, apparently a record of some accounts. 3 columns. 20 inches long by 10 inches high.

II. DEMOTIC AND GREEK PAPYRI.

The following twenty papyri (Nos. XLVI–LXVI), several of which are dated in the second and first century B.C., were found together in an earthen jar near Thebes. One of them is written in Greek uncials and three others in Demotic with Greek dockets: the remaining sixteen are written in Demotic only. The Demotic texts have not yet been examined, but they will form the subject of another volume. The Greek texts have been translated by Mr. B. P. Grenfell, from which translations the general character of the documents may be gathered. They were no doubt preserved as the title deeds of the property to which they refer.

PAPYRUS No. XLVI.

Demotic contract with a Greek docket, concerning certain taxes upon property, dated 11th day of Phaneroth in the XXXIst year of Ptolemy Euergetes II (Physcon), *i.e.*, 139 B.C.

PAPYRUS No. XLVII.

Demotic contract with a Greek docket, concerning certain taxes upon property, dated 3rd day of Pachon in the IIIrd year of Ptolemy Soter II (Lathyrus), *i.e.* 114 B.C.

PAPYRUS No. XLVIII.

Demotic contract with a Greek docket, concerning certain taxes upon property, dated in the 16th day of Mecheir in the fifth year of Ptolemy [Soter II (Lathyrus)], *i.e.*, 112 B.C.

PAPYRUS No. XLIX.

Papyrus written in Greek uncials, containing copies of official documents relating to certain taxes upon property. One of the documents contained in it is dated the 8th day of Choiach, in the VIth year of Cleopatra III and Ptolemy Soter II, *i.e.*, 112 B.C.

PAPYRUS No. L.

Demotic contract with docket also in demotic writing. Height of papyrus 12½ inches, length of roll 20 inches.

PAPYRUS No. LI.

Demotic contract with docket also in demotic writing. Height of papyrus 12 inches, length of roll 6 inches.

PAPYRUS No. LII.

Demotic contract. Height of papyrus 11¾ inches, length of roll 38 inches.

PAPYRI Nos. LIII–LXV.

Fourteen papyri of various sizes written in demotic, found together with Papyri Nos. XLVI–LII, and probably relating to the same subject. Ptolemaic.

I. GREEK PAPYRI.

PAPYRUS No. LXVI.

FRAGMENTS of a letter relating to the sale of a house. *Circa* 1st century B.C.

PAPYRUS No. LXVII.

FRAGMENT of a letter written in a very cursive character. *Circa* 5th century A.D.

PAPYRUS No. LXVIII.

FRAGMENT of a contract. *Circa* 5th century A.D.

PAPYRUS No. LXIX.

PAGE of accounts written in a very cursive character. *Circa* 8th century A.D.

J. COPTIC PAPYRI.

PAPYRUS No. LXX.

FRAGMENT of a letter found in the Fayúm. *Circa* 900 A.D

PAPYRUS No. LXXI.

FRAGMENT of a letter found in the Fayúm. *Circa* 900 A.D.

PAPYRUS No. LXXII.

WILL of Tsiblé, the daughter of Gapatios, written probably in the VIIIth century A.D. Mr. W. E. Crum has transcribed this document and translated it in full. His transcription, translation and notes are given as an appendix to the present volume. [See page 59.]

K. COPTIC AND ARABIC PAPYRI.

PAPYRI Nos. LXXIII–LXXVII.

FIVE letters written on the *recto* in Coptic and on the *verso* in Arabic. *Circa* 900 A.D.

PAPYRUS No. LXXVIII.

Two small fragments containing accounts written in Arabic. *Circa* 1000 A.D.

APPENDIX.

PAPYRUS No. LXXII.

BY

W. E. CRUM, M.A.

COPTIC PAPYRUS.

Composed of eight *selides*, in all 43¾ in. long by 6¼ in. wide. The text is written upon the horizontal fibres in a clumsy, ligatureless hand, probably of the eighth century. It consists of one of those numerous legal documents—over a hundred are at present known,—once deposited in the monastery of St. Phoebamon at 'Abd el-ḳurnah, the Jêmé of the Copts and their ancestors, the Castrum Memnonium of the Byzantines,—and now dispersed among the European museums. These documents fall for the most part into two groups; they are either dedications of children by their parents to the service of the monastery, or wills, sales and other declarations regarding ownership or inheritance. The present papyrus belongs to the latter group. It is written, like all the similar texts, in the Sa'idic dialect, with a heavy proportion of words drawn from the Greek documents upon which the Coptic legal terminology was modelled. The orthography of the whole is remarkably inaccurate.

The very unsystematic pointing of the original has been omitted in the following transcript; the spelling has not been corrected, and "*sic*" has been added at only a few points.

ϯ ϩⲙ ⲡⲣⲁⲛ ⲙⲡⲉⲓⲱⲧ ⲙⲛ ⲡϣⲏⲣⲉ ⲙⲛ ⲡⲉⲡⲛ̅ⲁ̅ ⲉⲧⲟⲩⲁⲁⲃ ϩⲙ ⲡⲟⲟⲩ ⲛϩⲟⲟⲩ ⲉⲧⲉⲥⲟⲩϫⲟⲩⲧⲏⲡⲉ ⲙⲡⲙⲉⲥⲟⲩⲣⲏ ⲛⲧⲉⲛⲧⲉⲣⲟⲙⲡⲉ (sic) ⲛⲧⲱⲧⲉⲕⲁⲧⲉⲥ ⲛⲧⲉⲕⲇⲓⲁⲛⲟⲥ ⲡⲁϩⲣⲛ ⲛⲧⲓⲙⲉⲓⲱⲧⲁⲧⲟⲥ | ⲗⲉⲟⲛⲧⲓⲟⲥ ⲙⲛ ⲙⲁⲙⲏⲛⲁ ⲡⲗⲁϣⲁⲛⲉ ⲙⲡⲕⲁⲥⲧⲣⲟⲛ ϫⲏⲙⲉ ⲁⲛⲟⲕ ⲧⲥⲓⲃⲗⲉ[2] ⲧϣⲏⲣⲉ ⲉⲛⲧⲁⲛⲁⲧⲓⲟⲥ[3] ϫⲉⲉⲛⲓⲧⲉ ⲁⲓϩⲏⲉ ⲁϩⲣⲁⲓ ⲁⲩϣⲱⲡⲉ ⲉϥϩⲟⲥⲉ ⲁⲓⲣϩⲟⲧⲉ ϫⲉⲙⲏⲡⲟⲧⲉ ⲛⲧⲉⲡⲛⲟⲩⲧⲉ ϣⲓⲛⲉ ⲛⲥⲱⲓ ⲛⲧⲁⲉⲓ ⲁⲃⲟⲗ ϩⲙ ⲡⲉ|ⲃⲓⲟⲥ ⲛⲧⲁⲕⲟ ⲙⲡⲁϩⲱⲃ ⲉϥϣⲡⲁⲛⲏⲥⲧⲟⲛ ⲙⲛⲧⲁⲡⲣⲱⲥⲫⲟⲣⲁ[4] ⲁⲓ[ϯ]ⲡⲗⲟⲩⲁⲓ ⲁⲇⲓⲁⲇⲓⲁⲑⲏⲕⲉ (sic) ⲉⲛⲁⲧⲡⲁⲣⲁⲃⲉ ⲙⲙⲟⲥ ⲛⲁⲧϣⲁⲗⲉⲥ ⲉⲃⲟⲗ ⲉⲡⲉⲣϩⲟⲟⲩⲟ ⲇⲉ ⲧⲁϫⲣⲟ ⲙⲙⲟⲥ ϩⲓⲧⲛ ϩⲛⲙⲉⲛⲧⲣⲏ ⲉⲛⲁⲝⲓⲟⲡⲓⲥⲧⲟⲥ | ⲁⲩⲱ ⲙⲡⲟⲩⲣⲉϥⲥϩⲁⲓ ⲉⲧⲣⲉϥⲥϩⲁⲓ ϩⲁⲣⲟⲟⲩ ⲉⲣⲉⲡⲁϩⲏⲧ ⲥⲙⲟⲛⲧ ⲉⲓϩⲙⲟⲟⲥ ϩⲓϫⲛⲡⲁⲙⲁⲛⲉⲛⲕⲟⲧⲉ ⲉⲣⲉⲡⲁⲛⲟⲥ ⲥⲙⲟⲛⲉⲧ ⲉⲣⲉⲡⲁⲗⲟⲅⲉⲥⲙⲟⲥ ⲧⲁϫⲣⲏⲩ ⲁⲓⲣϩⲟⲧⲉ ϫⲉⲙⲏⲡⲟⲧⲕ ⲛⲧⲉⲧⲁⲡⲟⲫⲁⲥⲓⲥ ⲧⲁϩⲟⲓ ϩⲱⲧ ⲡⲟⲥ | ⲛⲣⲱⲙⲉ ⲛⲓⲙ ⲕⲁⲧⲁⲑⲏ ⲛⲧⲁⲡⲛⲟⲩⲧⲉ ⲡⲗⲟⲅⲟⲥ ϩⲱⲣⲁⲍⲉ ⲙⲙⲟⲥ ⲁϫⲛⲡⲉⲛⲉⲓⲱⲧ ⲁⲇⲁⲙ ϫⲉⲛⲧⲕⲟⲩⲕⲁϩ ⲉⲕⲛⲁⲕⲟⲧⲉⲕ ⲁⲛⲕⲁϩ ⲁⲓⲧⲓⲡⲗⲟⲩⲁⲓ (sic) ⲇⲓⲁⲇⲓⲁⲑⲏⲕⲉ ⲉⲃⲟⲗϫⲉⲁⲓϩⲛⲉ ⲉⲛⲁϩⲁⲓ ⲉϥⲡⲣⲟⲥⲉⲭⲏ ⲁⲣⲟⲓ ϩⲙⲡⲁϩⲓⲥⲉ ⲧⲏⲣϥ | ⲁⲩⲱ ⲉϥⲫⲟⲗⲟⲕⲁⲣⲉ ⲁⲣⲟⲓ ϩⲙⲡⲙⲛⲧⲕⲁⲧⲁ[5] ⲛⲓⲙ ⲉϥⲉⲁⲗⲡⲉ ⲙⲙⲟⲓ ϩⲛⲧⲉϥϭⲟⲙ ⲧⲏⲣⲥ ⲁⲓϫⲟⲟⲥ ϫⲉⲙⲏⲡⲟⲩⲧⲉ ⲉⲛⲧⲉⲛⲟⲩⲧⲉ ϫⲡⲟⲓ ϩⲓⲡⲉϥⲃⲓⲙⲁ ⲉⲧϩⲁϩⲟⲧⲉ ⲉⲧⲃⲉⲡⲉϥϩⲓⲥⲉ ⲙⲛⲧⲁⲡⲣⲟⲥⲫⲟⲣⲁ ⲧⲉⲛⲟⲩⲧⲏ ϯⲕⲏⲗⲉⲩⲉ ⲛⲧⲉϩⲏ | ⲉⲧⲃⲉⲡⲉϥⲧⲟⲟⲩ ⲛⲧⲉⲣⲙⲏⲥⲥⲓⲟⲛ[6] ⲉⲣⲉⲡⲁϩⲁⲓ ⲛⲁⲃⲓⲧⲟⲩ ⲡⲉϥⲧⲁⲁⲩ ⲙⲡⲣⲟⲥⲫⲟⲣⲁ ϩⲁⲣⲟⲓ ⲁⲩⲱ ⲟⲛ ⲡⲁⲙⲉⲣⲟⲥ ⲉⲛⲏⲓ ⲛⲧⲁϥⲉⲓ ⲁϫⲱⲓ ϩⲁⲡⲁⲉⲓⲱⲧ ⲙⲡⲙⲁⲙⲏⲣⲟⲥ ⲡⲉⲱϩⲃⲉⲣⲃⲱⲧⲉ[7] ⲉⲣⲉⲡⲁϩⲁⲓ ⲡⲁϣⲱⲡⲉ ϥⲱ ⲛϫⲟⲉⲓⲥ ⲉⲣⲟⲟⲩ ⲉϥⲛⲁϫⲓⲧⲟⲩ | ϯⲙⲏⲛ ⲛⲧⲟⲧϥ ⲙⲡⲁⲥⲛⲏⲩ[5] ⲡⲉϥⲧⲁⲥ ⲙⲡⲟⲣⲟⲥⲫⲟⲣⲁ ϩⲁⲣⲟⲓ ⲁⲩⲱ ⲟⲛ ⲉⲧⲃⲉⲡⲉⲥⲕⲉⲩⲉ ⲛⲧⲁⲩⲉⲓ ⲁ[ϫⲱⲓ ϩ]ⲁⲡⲁⲉⲓⲱⲧ ⲉⲓⲱⲣⲕ ⲙⲡⲛⲟⲩⲧ[ⲉ[8] ⲡⲁⲛⲧ]ⲟⲕⲣⲁⲧⲱⲣ ϫⲉⲙⲉⲓϯⲗⲁⲩⲉ ⲙⲡⲁϩⲁⲓ ⲛϩⲏⲧⲟⲩ ⲙⲡⲉⲗⲁⲩⲉ ⲛⲣⲱⲙⲉ ⲉϥϭⲙϭⲟⲙ ⲉⲛⲉⲓ ⲁ|ⲃⲟⲗ ⲁⲣⲟⲕ ϣⲁⲁⲛⲉϩ ⲉϩⲁⲗⲁⲩⲉ ⲙⲡⲣⲟⲫⲁⲥⲓⲥ ⲛⲇⲓⲙⲉⲓⲛⲉ ⲟⲩⲧⲉ ⲥⲟⲛ ⲟⲩⲧⲉ ⲥⲱⲛⲉ ⲟⲩⲧⲉ ⲣⲱⲙⲉ ϩⲱⲗⲉⲥ ⲉⲛϣⲓⲛⲉ ⲟⲩⲧⲉ ⲛⲧⲟⲕ ⲟⲩⲧⲉ

ⲡⲉⲧⲛⲏⲩ ⲧⲏⲣⲟⲩ ⲙⲛ̄ⲛⲥⲱⲥ ⲕⲁⲛ ⲧⲓⲛⲟⲩ ⲕⲁⲛ ϣⲁⲟⲩⲟⲉⲓϣ ⲛⲓⲙ ⲡⲉⲧ|ⲛⲁⲧⲱⲗⲙⲁ ⲉⲡⲁⲣⲁⲃⲉ ⲛ̄ⲇⲓⲁⲑⲏⲕⲉ ⲟⲩⲧⲉ ϣⲙⲙⲟ ⲟⲩⲧⲉ ⲣⲱⲙⲉ ⲉⲡⲱⲓⲛⲉ ⲉⲧⲃⲉ ⲧⲁⲡⲣⲟⲥⲫⲟⲩⲣⲁ ⲙⲛ̄ⲛⲁⲛⲁϣ ⲛ̄ⲧⲁⲓⲟⲣⲉⲕⲛϥ ⲁⲗⲗⲁ ⲉⲣⲉⲡⲁϩⲁⲓ ⲛⲁϣⲱⲡⲉ ⲉϥⲟ ⲛ̄ϫⲟⲉⲓⲥ ⲁϫⲛ̄ⲧⲁⲡⲣⲟⲥⲫⲟⲣⲁ ⲧⲏⲣⲉⲥ ϩⲛ̄ⲟⲟⲧⲉ | ⲛ̄ⲛⲟⲩⲧⲉ ⲉϥⲛⲁⲧⲓⲛⲕⲉ ⲙⲙⲟⲥ ϫⲉⲙⲡⲉⲗⲁⲩⲉ ⲛ̄ⲣⲱⲙⲉ ⲉϣϭⲙϭⲟⲙ ⲛ̄ⲇⲓⲕⲉ ⲙⲙⲟⲥ ⲛ̄ⲥⲁⲃⲉⲗⲗⲏϥ ⲉⲓⲱⲣⲕ ⲙ̄ⲡⲛⲟⲩⲧⲉ ⲡⲁⲛⲧⲟⲩⲕⲣⲁⲧⲱⲣ ϫⲉ ⲗⲁⲩⲉ ⲉⲡⲁⲣⲭⲟⲛ ⲛⲓⲙ ϩⲓⲗⲁϣⲁⲛⲉ ϩⲓⲧⲏⲡⲟⲥ ⲛⲓⲙ ⲉϥϩⲁⲉⲓⲟⲟⲩ | ⲉⲧⲟⲟϣⲉⲧ ⲙⲁϥ ⲉϥⲛⲁϫⲱⲙⲉϥ [10] ⲁⲇⲓⲁⲑⲏⲕⲉ ⲉⲧⲣⲉϥϩⲁⲣⲏϩ ⲁⲣⲟⲥ ⲕⲁⲧⲁ ⲟⲛ ⲉⲧⲥⲏϩ ϫⲉⲉⲛϩⲓⲥⲧⲓ ⲛⲁⲓ ⲉⲧⲣⲁⲣⲡⲉⲓⲧⲉϩⲛⲁⲓ ϩⲙⲡⲓⲧⲉⲡⲱⲓⲛⲉ ⲡⲉⲧⲛⲁⲧⲱⲗⲙⲁ ⲉⲡⲁⲣⲁⲃⲉ ⲙⲙⲟⲥ ⲛ̄ϣⲟⲣⲉⲡ ⲙⲉⲛ ⲛⲛⲉ|ⲡⲉⲧⲙⲙⲁⲩ ⲧⲓϩⲏⲧ ⲛⲗⲁⲉ ⲁⲗⲗⲁ ⲛ̄ϣⲟⲣⲉⲡ ⲛ̄ⲧⲏⲡⲟⲥ [11] ⲙⲙⲛ ⲉϥⲛⲁϣⲱⲡⲉ ⲉϥⲟ ⲛ̄ϣⲙⲙⲟ ⲉⲡⲁⲛⲁϣ ⲉⲧ[ⲟ]ⲩⲁⲁⲃ ⲉⲧ[ⲟⲩϣⲙ]ϣⲉ ⲙⲁϥ ⲡⲉⲓⲱⲧ [ⲙ]ⲛ̄ⲡϣⲏⲣⲉ ⲙⲛ̄ⲡⲛⲁⲩ[ⲙ]ⲁ ⲉⲧⲟⲩⲁⲁⲃ ⲁⲩⲱ ⲟⲛ ⲉϥⲛⲁϯⲡⲗⲟⲅⲟⲥ | ⲛ̄ϣⲟⲙⲉⲧ ⲉ[ⲛ]ⲟⲛⲧⲓⲁ [12] ⲛ̄ⲛⲟϭ ⲛⲉⲥⲁⲡⲏⲧⲉ ⲙⲙ[ⲟ]ϥ ϩⲛ̄ⲧⲉϥϩⲩⲡⲟⲥⲧⲁⲥⲓⲥ ⲙⲛ̄ⲛⲥⲱⲥ ⲛ̄ⲥⲉⲡⲁⲣⲁⲥⲕⲉⲩⲉⲍⲉ ⲙⲙⲟϥ ⲧⲁⲣⲉϥϩⲱⲛ ⲁⲧϭⲟⲙ ⲛ̄ⲧⲓⲇⲓⲁⲑⲏⲕⲉ ⲙⲛ̄ⲧⲥⲓⲙⲓⲁ [13] ⲛ̄ⲛⲗⲁϣⲁⲛⲉ ⲛ̄ⲛⲕⲏⲣⲟⲥ ⲉⲧⲙⲙⲁⲩ ⲧⲓ|ⲇⲓⲁⲑⲏⲕⲉ ⲟⲩⲛ ⲉⲥⲛⲁϣⲱⲡⲉ ⲉⲥⲧⲁϫⲣⲏ[ⲩ]

ⲁⲛⲟⲕ ⲧⲥⲓⲃⲗⲉ ⲧⲉⲛⲧⲁⲥϣⲣⲡⲥϩⲁⲓ ⲧⲡⲉⲥⲧⲏⲭⲏ ⲁⲧⲓⲇⲓⲁⲑⲏⲕⲉ ⲙⲛ̄ϩⲱⲃ ⲛⲓⲙ ⲉϥⲥⲏϩ ⲁⲣⲟⲥ ⲉⲃⲟϫⲉⲁⲩⲟⲩⲱϣⲉⲥ ⲁⲣⲟⲓ ⲁⲓⲥⲟⲧⲙⲉⲥ ⲉⲙⲉⲛⲧⲣⲙⲛ̄ⲕⲏⲙⲉ | ⲁⲩⲱ ⲟⲛ ⲁⲓⲡⲁⲣⲁⲕⲁⲗⲉ ⲛⲟⲩⲣⲉϥⲥϩⲁⲓ ⲙⲛ̄ϩⲉⲛⲕⲟⲩⲙⲛ̄ⲧⲣⲉ ⲉⲧⲣⲉⲙⲙⲁⲣⲧⲩⲣⲉⲥⲟⲁⲓ ϩⲁⲣⲟⲓ ⲁⲓⲕⲟⲥ ⲁⲃⲟⲗ ⲱⲥ ⲛ̄ⲣⲱⲕⲉⲧⲏ +

⳨ [14] ⲁⲛⲟⲕ ⲁⲛⲧⲣⲉⲁⲥ ⲡϣⲏⲣⲉ ⲙⲡⲙⲁⲕⲁⲣⲓⲟⲥ ⲫⲟⲃⲁⲙⲙⲱⲛ ϯⲟ ⲙⲙⲛ̄ⲧⲣⲉ

⳨ ⲁⲛⲟⲕ [ⲅⲉ]ⲱⲣⲅⲓⲟⲥ ⲡϣⲏⲣⲉ ⲙⲡⲙⲁⲕ, ⲥⲁ[ⲙⲟⲩ]ⲏⲗ ϯⲟ ⲙⲙⲛ̄ⲧⲣⲉ

⳨ ⲁⲛⲟⲕ [illegible] ⲡϣⲏⲣⲉ ⲙⲡⲙⲁⲕ, ⲯⲁⲛ ϯⲟ ⲙⲙⲛ̄ⲧⲣⲉ

ⲁⲛⲟⲕ . ⲉⲱ . ⲓⲥⲧⲟⲥ ⲡⲁⲛⲁⲅⲛⲱⲥⲧⲏⲥ ⲡⲁⲡⲁ ⲕⲩⲣⲓⲁⲕⲟⲥ [15] ⲁⲓⲥϩⲁⲓ ϩⲁⲣⲱⲟⲩ ϫⲉ|ⲙⲉⲩⲛⲟⲓ ⲛ̄ⲥϩⲁⲓ +

⳨ ⲁⲛⲟⲕ ⲥⲉⲩⲏⲣⲟⲥ ⲡϣⲏⲣⲉ ⲙⲡⲙⲁⲕⲁⲣⲉⲓⲟⲥ ⲥⲁⲙⲟⲩⲏⲗ ⲁⲓⲥϩⲁⲓ ⲛ̄ⲧⲉⲧⲓⲁⲑⲏⲕⲉ ⲛ̄ⲧⲁϭⲓϫ ⲡⲣⲟⲥ ⲧⲏⲧⲓⲥⲓⲥ ⲙⲡⲉⲧⲥⲙⲓⲛⲉ ⲙⲙⲟⲥ +

Translation.

In the name of the Father and the Son and the Holy Ghost (πνευμα)! Upon this day, which is the 25th day of Mesore, in this year of the 12th (δωδεκατος) Indiction (ινδικτιων); before the most honourable (τιμιωτατος) | Leontios and Mena, magistrates of the township (καστρον) Jêmé;

I, Tsiblé, the daughter of Gapatios, since (επειδη) I have fallen into a serious (*lit.* troublesome) malady, I have been afraid lest (μηποτε) God should seek after me and I should depart out of this | life (βιος) and leave my property uncared-for (ṛeuḷ απρονοητος) and my offering (προσφορα), I have had recourse (therefore) to this testament (διαθηκη), untransgressable (παραβαινειν), indissoluble; (and) we (*sic*) have further confirmed it by means of trustworthy (αξιοπιστος) witnesses, | and with a scribe to write on their behalf; (and this) while my mind is fixed, as I sit upon my bed, my understanding (νους) being steadfast and my reason (λογισμος) firm. For I was afraid lest (μηποτε) the decree (αποφασις) reach me also, like | all men, even as (κατα) God the Word (λογος) enjoined upon our common father, Adam, saying, Earth art thou; to the earth shalt thou return.

I have had recourse to this testament (διαθηκη) because I have recognized that my husband devotes himself (προσεχειν) to me in all my business | and looks to my interest (φιλοκαλειν) in all service, cherishing (θαλπειν) me with all his power. (And) I said, lest God question me at his fearful tribunal (βημα) concerning his (*i.e.*, my husband's) trouble and my offering (προσφορα);

So (γε) now I do order (κελευειν) in this wise | regarding the four trimesia (τριμησιον); my husband shall take them and shall give them as an offering (προσφορα) on my behalf. And moreover, my portion (μερος) of a house, that came to me from my father, and my portion (μερος) of a —? field, my husband shall be master of them; he shall get their | price (τιμη) from my brethren and shall give it as an offering (προσφορα). And further, as to the chattels (σκευη) which have come to me from my father, I swear to God Almighty (παντοκρατωρ) that I will not give (*or*, am not giving) anything of them to my husband.

There shall no man ever have power to sue | thee upon any pretext (προφασις), as follows; neither (ουτε) brother nor (ουτε) sister nor (ουτε) any relative (*lit.* man) at all (ολως) of mine; neither (ουτε) thee nor (ουτε) any of those that come after thee, whether (καν) it be now or (καν) at any time. He that | shall dare (τολμαν) to transgress (παραβαινειν) this testament (διαθηκη), whether (ουτε) stranger or relative (*lit.* man) of mine, concerning my offering (προσφορα) and the oath that I have sworn,—But (αλλα) my husband shall be master over my whole offering (προσφορα) in the fear | of God; he shall administer (διοικειν) it, so that no man shall have power to administer (διοικειν) it excepting him. I conjure by God Almighty (παντοκρατωρ) every governor (αρχων) and magistrate and every honourable, | worshipful personage (τυπος) who shall happen upon (?) this testament (διαθηκη), that he keep it, according as (κατα) it is written that it is lawful (εξεστι) for me to do what pleases me with mine own.

He that shall dare (τολμαν) to transgress (παραβαινειν) it, firstly (+ μεν), that man shall | not prosper in anything; but (αλλα, μεν) in the first place (τυπος), he shall be estranged from the holy oath which men (*lit.* they) serve, (from) the Father, the Son and the Holy Ghost (πνευμα); and also he shall pay the amount (λογος) | of three ounces (ογγια) of gold and they shall receive (απαιτειν) it from his property (υποστασις). Afterwards they shall see to it (παρασκευαζειν) that he conform to the authority of this testament (διαθηκη) and the penalty (*read* επιτιμια) of the magistrate of that time (καιρος). This | testament (διαθηκη) therefore (ουν) shall be established.

I, Taiblé, that wrote above, do agree to (στοιχειν) this testament (διαθηκη) and to all things that are written in it; for they have read it to me (and) I have heard it in the Egyptian (tongue). | And moreover I have called in (παρακαλειν) a scribe and witnesses besides, that they might bear witness (μαρτυρεσθαι) for me (and) I have published it as it is set forth (ως προκειται).

I, Andreas, the son of the deceased (μακαριος) Phoebamon, am witness.

| I, Georgios, the son of the deceased (μακαριος) so Samuel, am witness.

I, —?, the son of the deceased (μακαριος) Psan, am witness.

I, Theopistos (?), the reader (αναγνωστης) of (the church of) Apa Kyriakos, have written for them, for | they know (νοειν) not (how) to write.

I, Severus, the son of the deceased (μακαριος) Samuel, have written this testament (διαθηκη) with my hand, at (προς) the request (αιτησις) of her who authorized it.

Notes.

[1] Unfortunately none of the persons in this text—magistrates, witnesses, scribe,—recur in other similar MSS. Twelfth Indictions fall, *e.g.*, in A.D. 729, 744, 759, 774, 789.

[2] ⲧⲥⲓⲃⲗⲉ occurs also in the 2nd Boulak papyrus. *Cf.* Bodleian, MS. Copt. (P), c. 4, ⲧⲥⲓⲃⲏⲗ.

[3] Read perhaps ⲡⲁⲡⲁⲇⲓⲟⲥ, a frequent name.

[4] The ⲡⲣⲟⲥⲫⲟⲣⲁ consists in these texts of the person of the child to be dedicated, of the person of the testator himself, of cattle, palm-trees, or, as here, of money.

[5] For ⲁⲁⲛⲧϭⲁⲧⲟⲛ.

[6] The τριμήσιον was the 3rd of the νόμισμα, (solidus, ϩⲟⲗⲟⲕⲟⲧⲧⲓⲛⲟⲥ.)

[7] A word of uncertain meaning; *v. Aeg. Zeitschr.*, 1869, 131.

[8] "From my brethren" was inserted later, above the line.

[9] There is not space in the gap for two ⲛ's (*cf.* l. 52).

[10] A word of doubtful meaning; *v. Aeg. Zeitschr.*, 1871, 46.

[11] *Cf.* the corresponding Greek expression πρωτοτύπως.

[12] The ounce (since Justinian) = $\frac{1}{12}$ of 72 solidi (1 libra), *i.e.* = 6 solidi.

[13] No doubt this is the extra penalty, ἐπιτιμία, of Brit. Mus., Or. 4868, 4871, 4872, &c.

[14] Ll. 78–85 are in the hand of the "scribe" whom Taiblé had engaged (l. 15).

[15] This church is mentioned in Brit. Mus., Or. 1061 C. and Pap. 105 (*Rev. ég.* I, 101).

LIST OF PLATES.

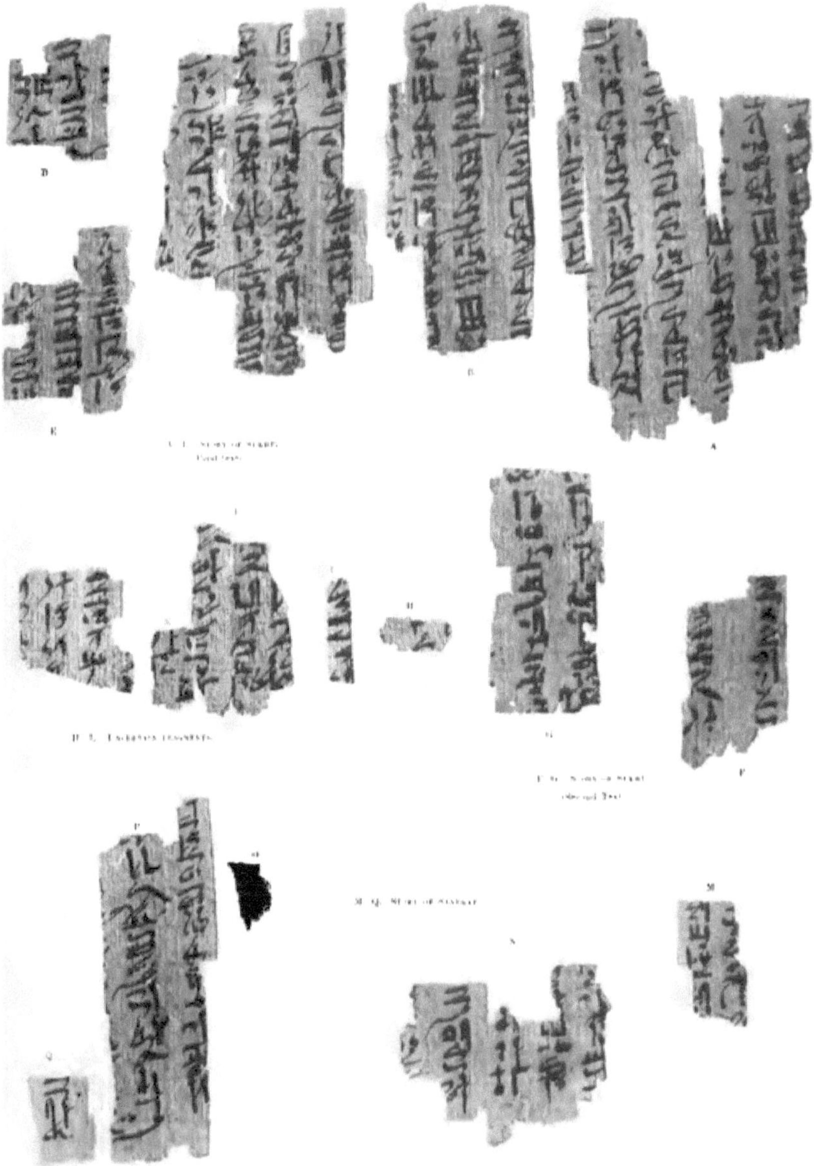

EARLY LITERARY FRAGMENTS

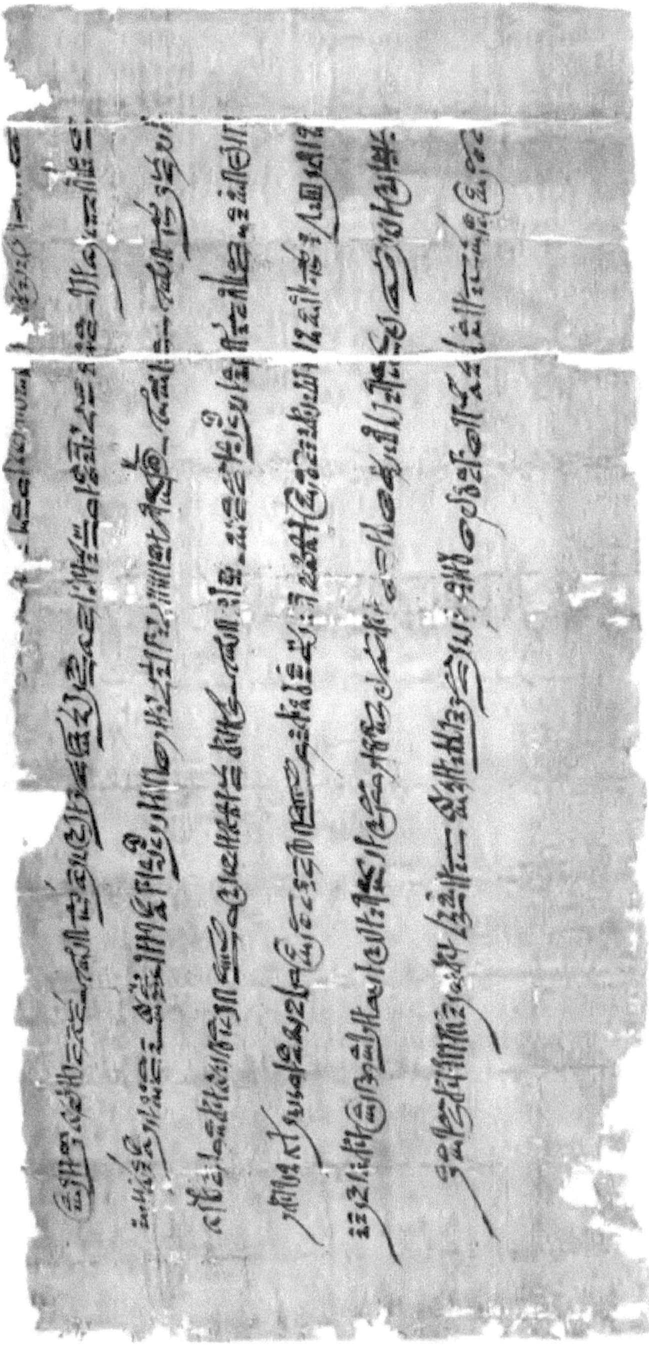

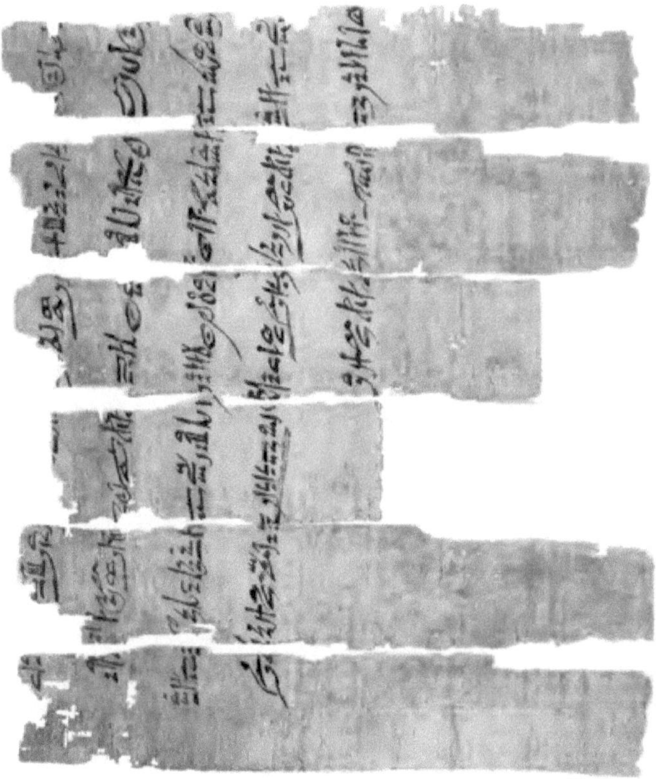

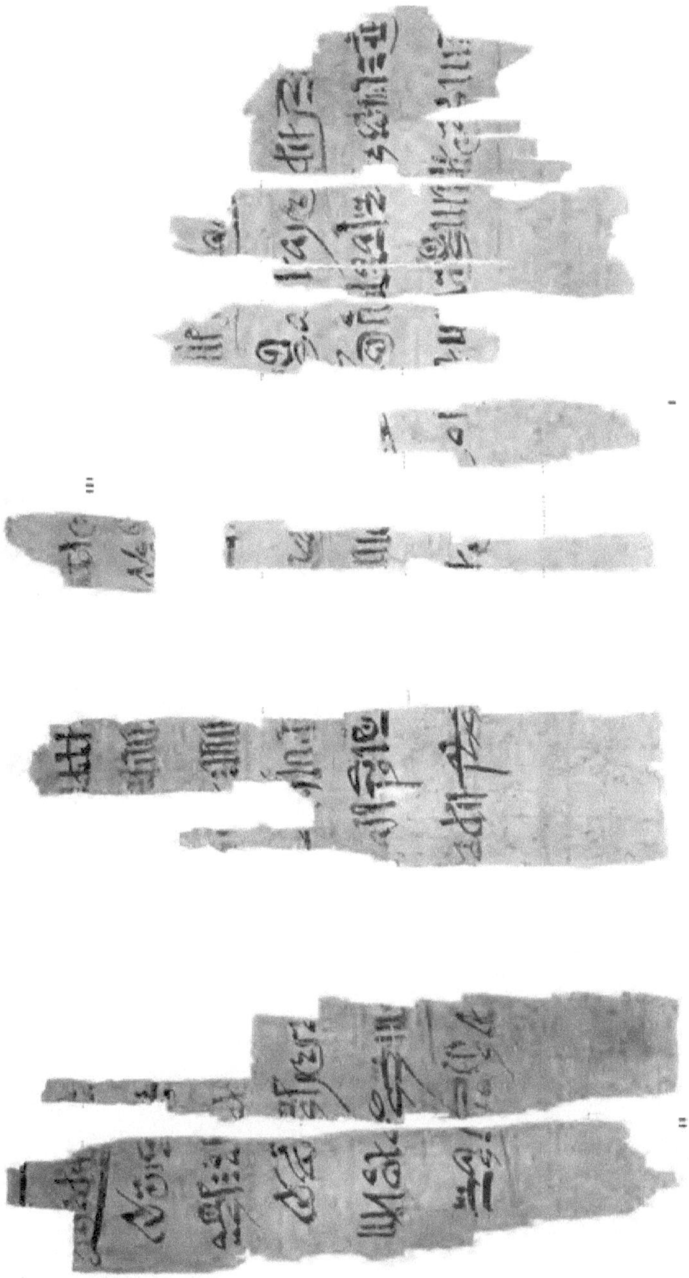

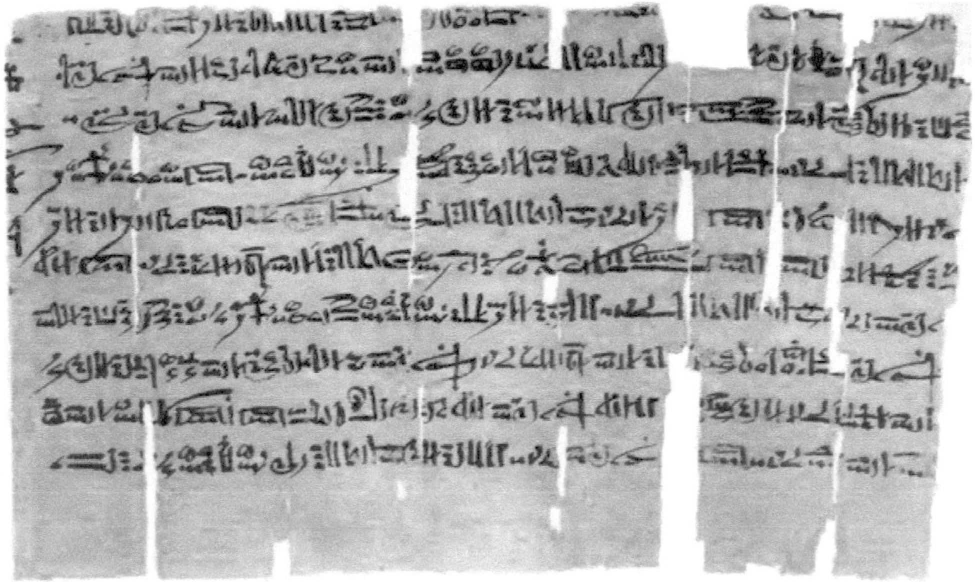

THE AMHERST PAPYRUS (II)

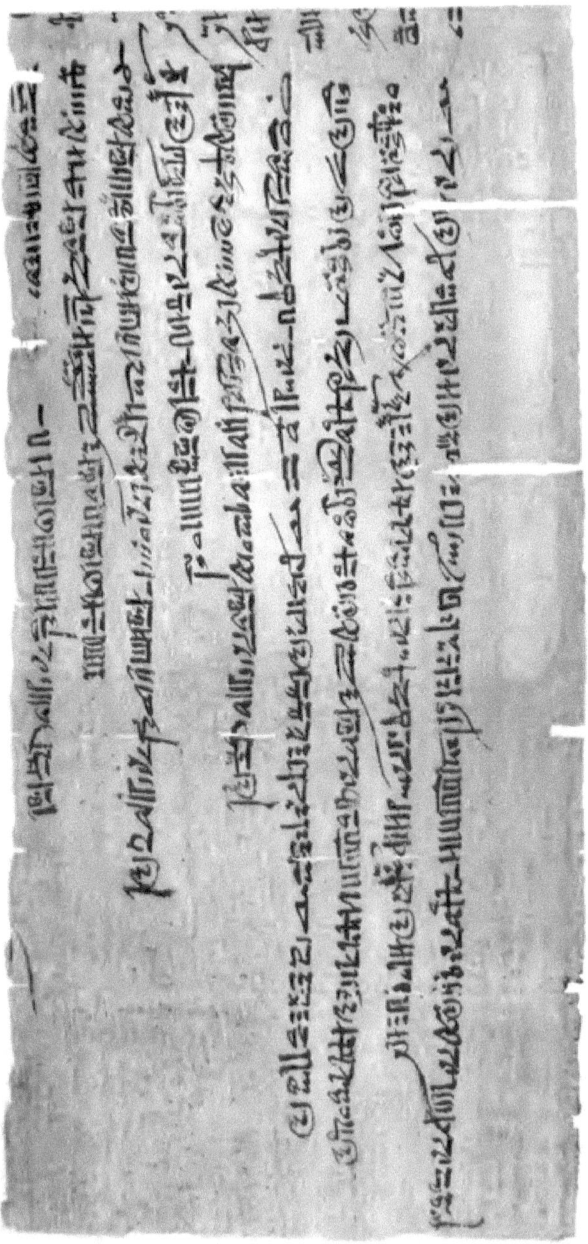

THE AMHERST PAPYRUS (IV)

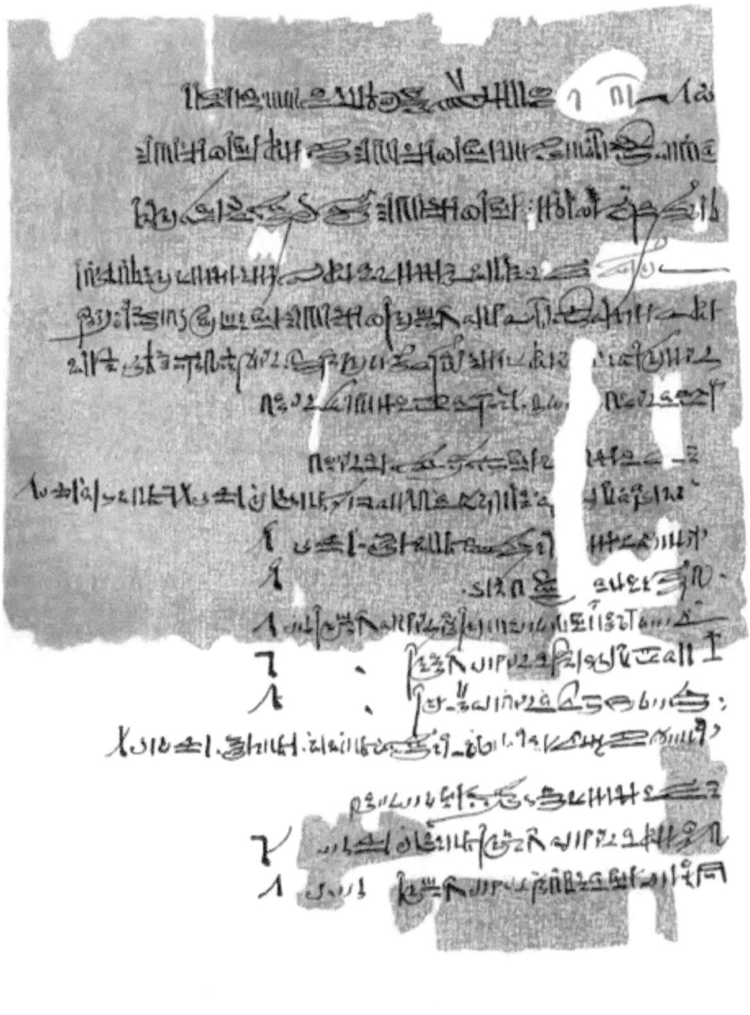

THE HARRIS PAPYRUS A. (I).

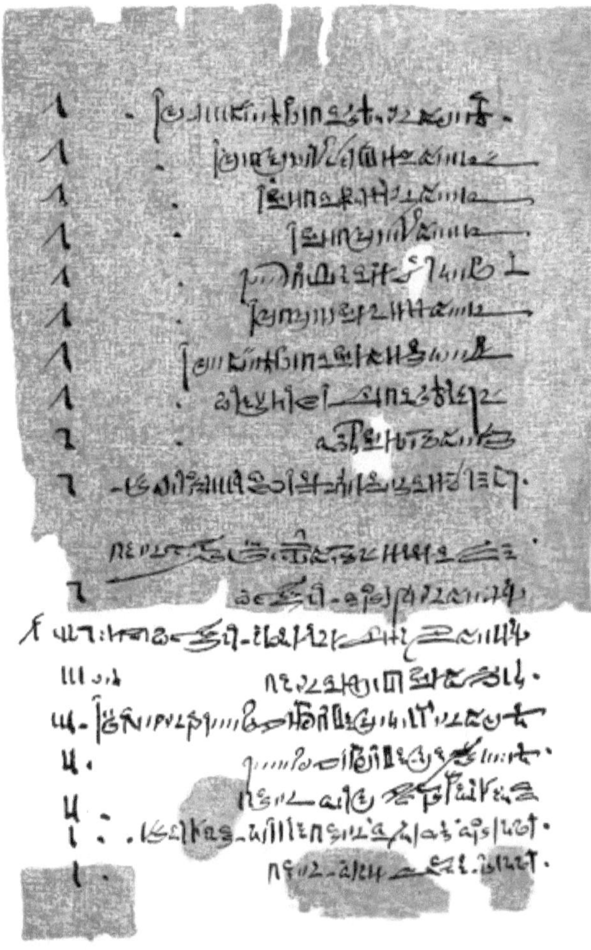

THE HARRIS PAPYRUS A. (II).

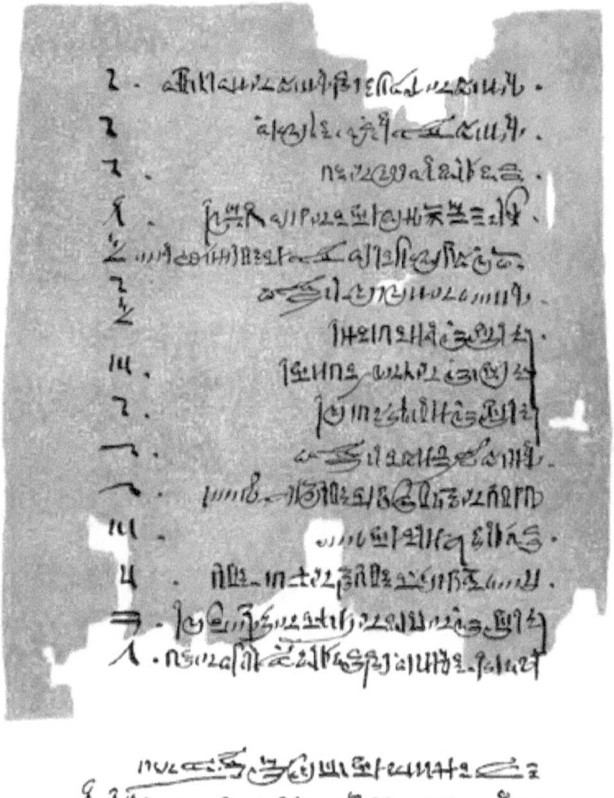

THE HARRIS PAPYRUS A. (III).

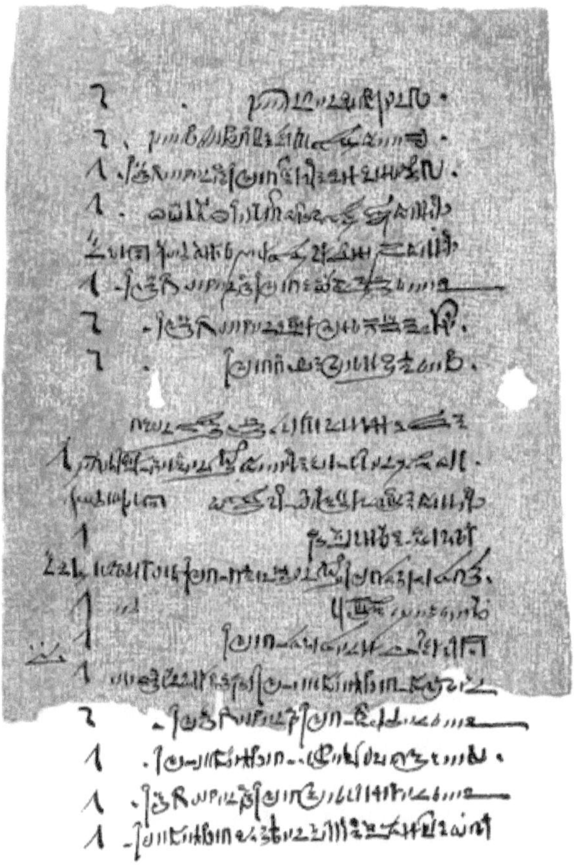

THE HARRIS PAPYRUS A. (IV).

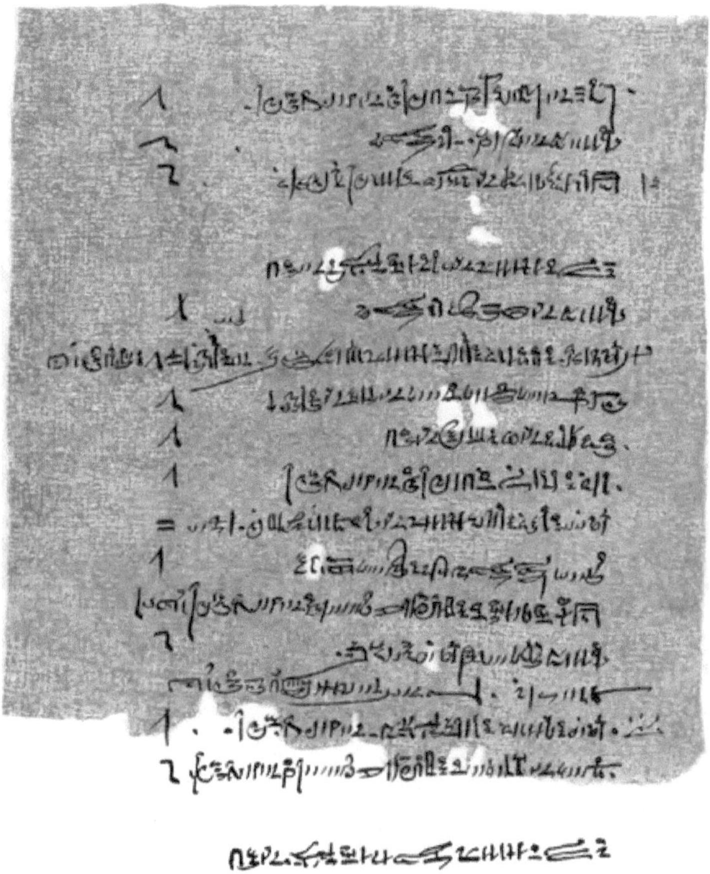

THE HARRIS PAPYRUS A. (V).

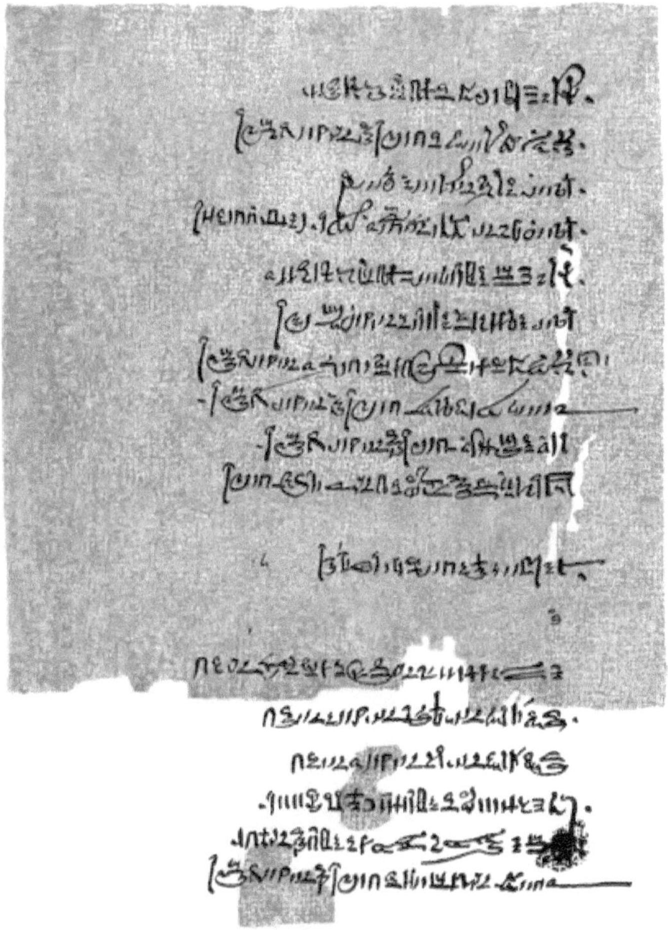

THE HARRIS PAPYRUS A. (VI).

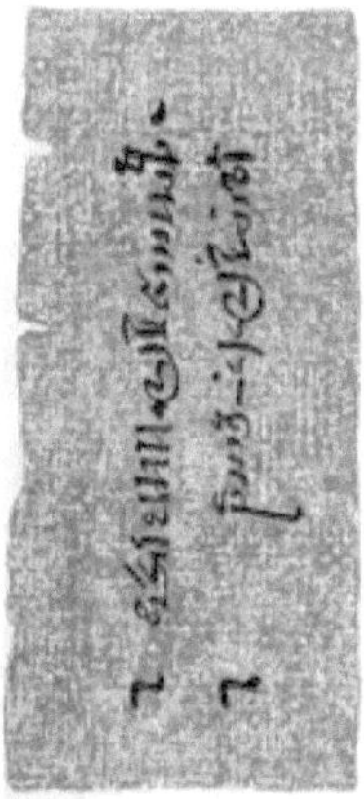

VIII.

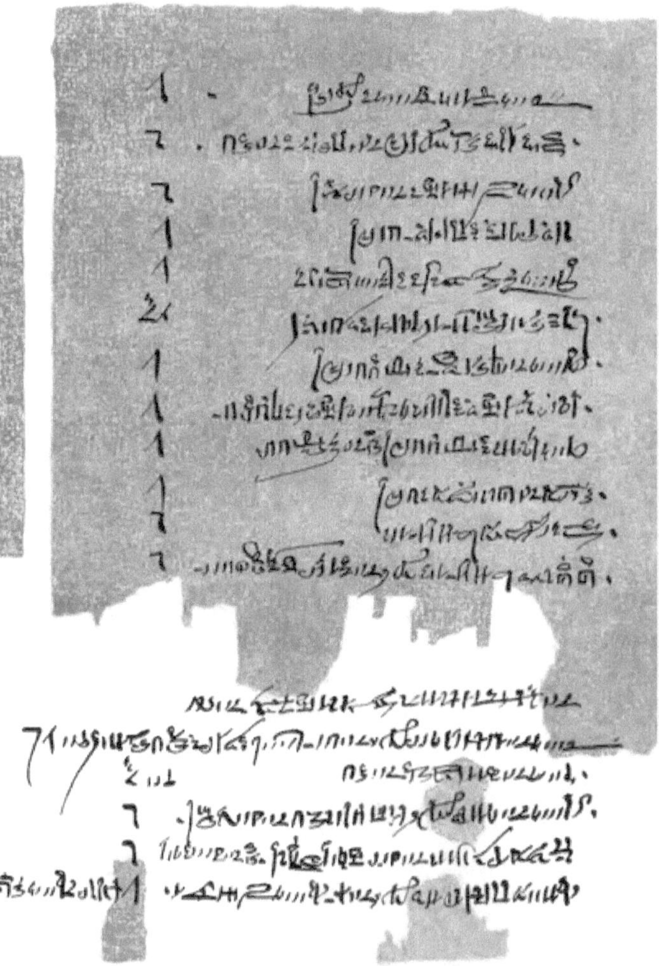

VII.

THE HARRIS PAPYRUS A. (VII & VIII).

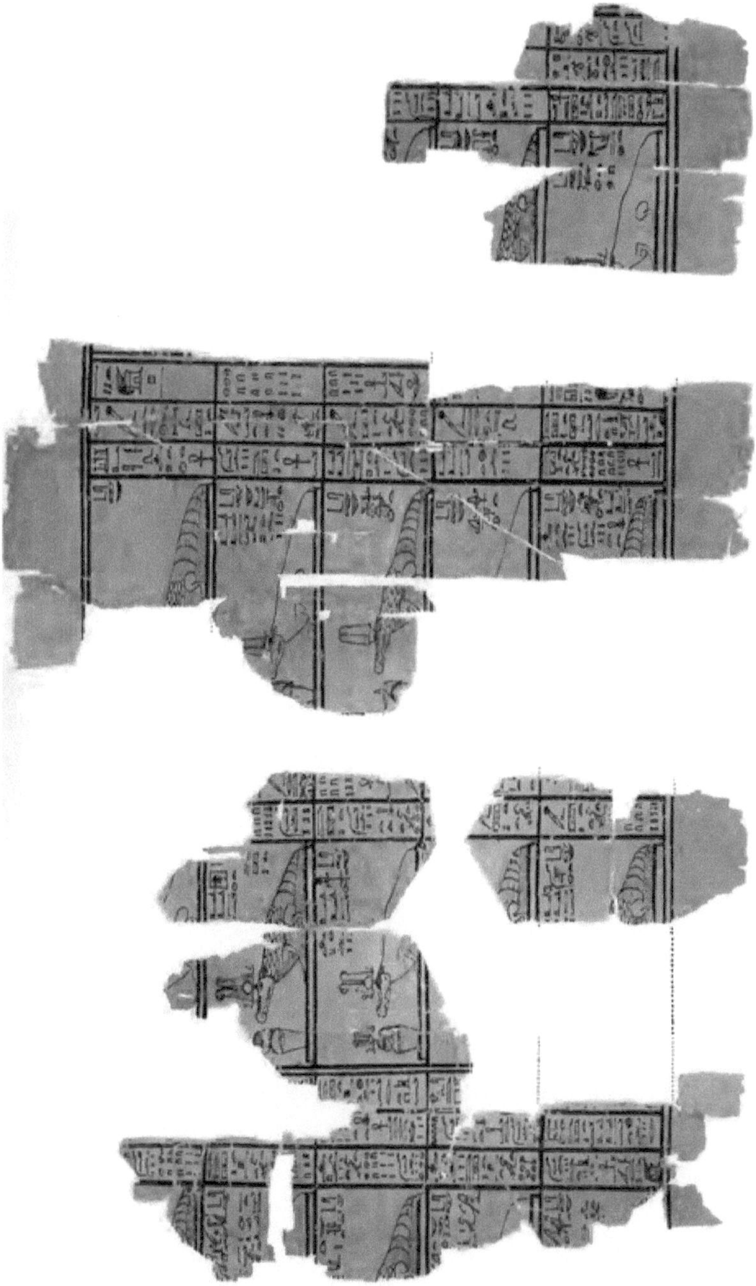

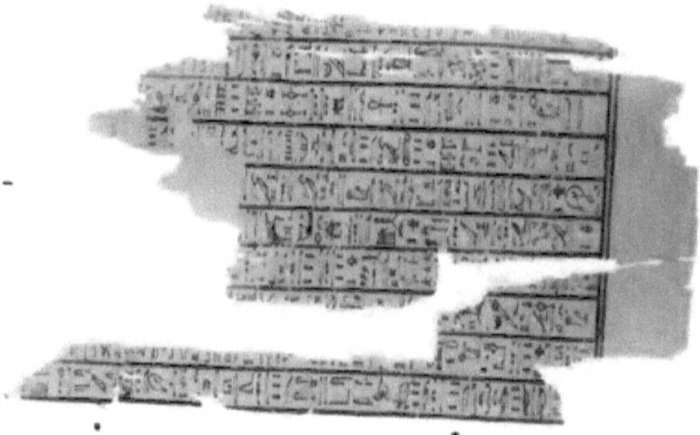

I
II
III
IV
V
VI
VII

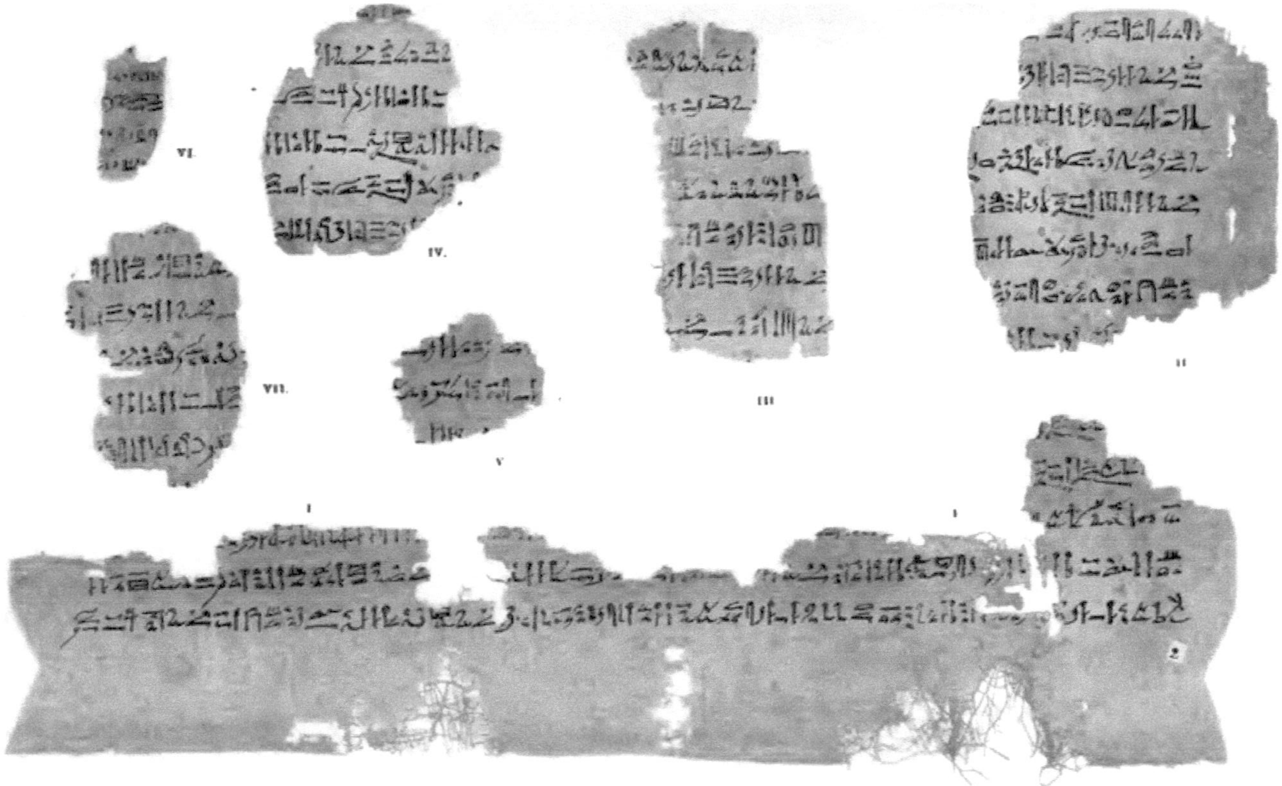

VI.
IV.
VII.
V
III
II
I
I

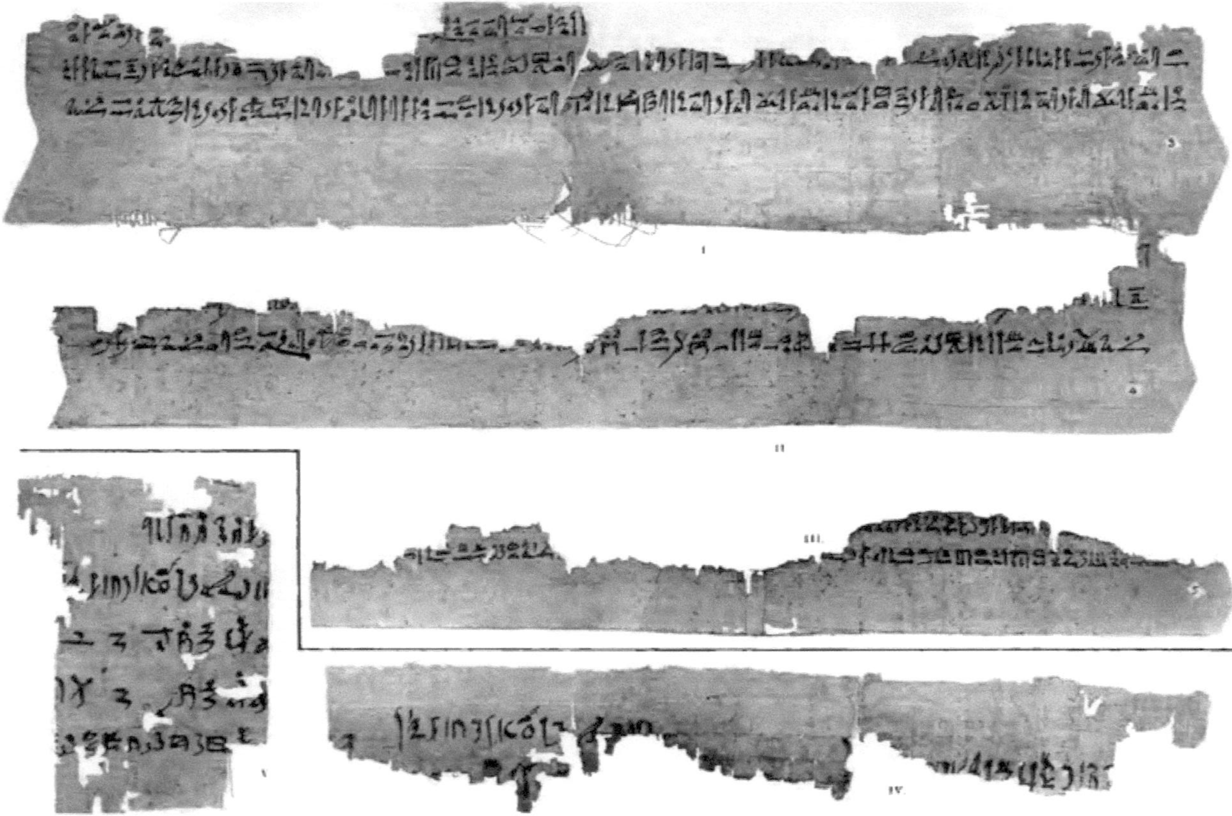

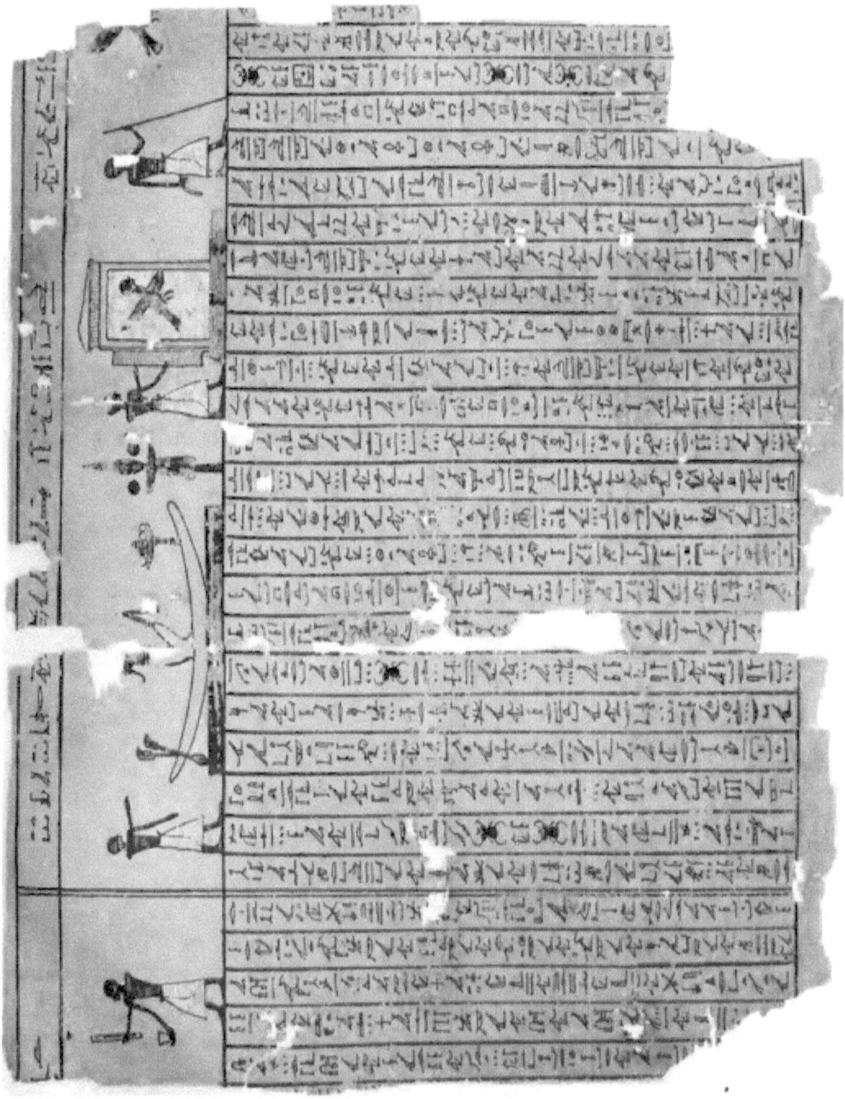

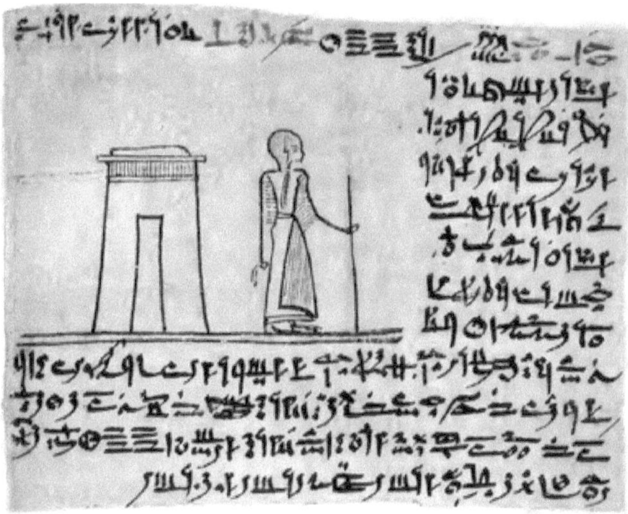

THE PAPYRUS OF HOR-NEST-ATEF-EF.

www.ingramcontent.com/pod-product-compliance
Lightning Source LLC
Chambersburg PA
CBHW030406170426
43202CB00010B/1515
9783337243302